YOUR KNOWLEDGE HAS VALUE

Artificial Intelligence in order to facilitate Diagnoses and Treatment. The Opportunity Smart Cities give Subjects

Sina Kiene

Bibliographic information published by the German National Library:

The German National Library lists this publication in the National Bibliography; detailed bibliographic data are available on the Internet at http://dnb.dnb.de.

ISBN: 9783346397669
This book is also available as an ebook.

© GRIN Publishing GmbH
Nymphenburger Straße 86
80636 München

Print and binding: Books on Demand GmbH, Norderstedt, Germany
Printed on acid-free paper from responsible sources.

The present work has been carefully prepared. Nevertheless, authors and publishers do not incur liability for the correctness of information, notes, links and advice as well as any printing errors.

GRIN web shop: https://www.grin.com/document/994741

Macromedia
University of Applied Sciences

BACHELOR THESIS
Final paper for the obtainment of the
Bachelor of Arts Degree

"Smart Cities give subjects the opportunity to use
Artificial Intelligence in order to facilitate diagnoses
and treatment"
in the course of study Media Management
study focus Media and Communication Management

Submitted by: Sina Kiene

Course of study: Media Management
Study focus: Media and Communication Management

Wentorf bei Hamburg, 28.01.2020

Abstract

Nowadays society faces challenges in several sectors, because of the shift in society, the growing use of technology as well as rising health issues. Therefore, this bachelor thesis is based on the approach of providing nowadays society with solutions through the advancement of Artificial Intelligence in order to improve their quality of life. For the reason that the obstacles within the health sector are evolving in a negative sense a special focus within this concept is laid on Artificial Intelligence systems impact within the health sector of mental illnesses. Thus being said the structure of the thesis focuses on four key theories in the beginning which arise over and over within the thesis. These four key theories included: The Wave Approach by Toeffler, the definition of three identities, Neuroscience and Mental Illnesses (burn-out, depression and anxiety). Nevertheless, the thesis was examined in several other parts such as Artificial Intelligence and the technology behind it, the implementation of AI in smart cities, pattern recognition and monitoring in the health sector.

By focusing on such areas, analysing and connecting them with past approaches the impact of the data was described and analysed. Thus being said the thesis approach was coming to the conclusion that through the implementation of Artificial Intelligence systems such as voice recognition systems and facial recognition systems the area of diagnosing mental illnesses and improving treatment as well as reaching for quicker response rate — in regards to emergencies — can be reached.

Acknowledgements

Finishing my bachelor degree was a three and a half years journey with a lot of people who stayed close to my side during all these years and making this graduation happen. Therefore, I like to take the opportunity to especially thank my parents and grandparents who did not only supported me during this time financially but also by motivating and rooting for me, my successes and my path ahead. In this setting I also like to thank my younger sister who held up my spirit during stressful times even though she had to study as well. Without you five I would never have been able to finish my degree.

Additionally, I like to thank my research supervisor Prof. Dr. Thomas Santoro. Without their assistance and availability of support in every step through the process — when it was needed— this research paper would miss essentials. Thank you so much for your support over the stressful time of the bachelor thesis, all the ideas and additional books and recommendations.

I would also like to thank Dr. Okan Tansu. Without their inspirational spirit and innovative thinking, I would never have focused on the subject of AI, emotional reading etc.. So, thank you for not only inspiring me but also believing in my futuristic ideas and giving me new and fresh perceptions to the layers of media and communication.

Last but not least I like to thank: Michael Dehm, Nicoletta Blaschke and Lothar Hotz. Without their open mind and agreement of being interviewed the important part of expert interview would be miss from my thesis. Thank you for being so kind and open minded — spending a lot of time with me to generate new important insights — helping to support my thesis and hypotheses.

Key Words

Artificial Intelligence

The Era of AI

Monitoring

Emotions

Mental Illnesses

Health Sector

Table of Contents

List of Abbreviation

Abbreviation	Full word
AI	Artificial Intelligence
IoT	Internet of Things
ML	Machine Learning
NL	Neuro Learning
DL	Deep Learning
MIT	Massachusetts Institute of Technology
Gen Z	Generation Z
p.	Page
pp.	Pages
Fig.	Figure
NAMI	National Alliance on Mental Illness
NLP	Natural Language Processing

1.0 Introduction

In order to introduce the topic of this bachelor's thesis, which can be described as a scientific research paper, some general information have to be pointed too. The following section will focus on this aspect and create an overview of the thesis topic.

1.1 Background Information

By focusing on the implementation of artificial intelligence (AI) in the sector of health, several opportunities to dive deep into the topic arose. For this reason, it was decided to put the center of attention towards the subjects' mental health issues. In order to reflect this approach, a research question was developed.

"How can Artificial Intelligence monitoring aid in the improvement of the quality of life in today's society? "

1.2 Thesis Topic

As the topic of AI and its impact on life improvement covers a significant number of aspects, including the Internet of Things (IoT), emotions, and neuroscience, as well as smart devices and data analysis — it was decided to implement several theories. That includes the presentation of the approach of the Third Wave by Toffler (1980), three different identities, and emotion recognition were used to identify possible conclusions to the research question.

It is believed that through the use of AI, the quality of life of human society can be improved. Specifically, in the health sector focusing on depression detection and improvement of therapy settings (including suicide and anxiety), Through the fast-evolving smart society and smart cities, new possibilities for society open up, making its life more comfortable.

1.3 Thesis & Hypotheses

Taking these approaches into account, the decision was made to create a thesis statement, which will be analysed upon the following researched in the upcoming chapters.

"Through the influence of Artificial Intelligence, smart technology, and the Internet of Things, the quality of life can be improved."

When focusing on this specific statement, several more assumptions in regards to the topic of AI and its impact on life can be made. Especially within the health sector in regards to mental health — which started to be a popular topic in recent years triggered the decision to create four hypotheses — in order to reinforce the thesis statement and conduct research on a deeper level.

Hypothesis 1	New technologies originally created the issue of anxiety, burn-out and depression but now has the potential to create solutions
Hypothesis 2	Monitoring health concerns via current technology increases the probability for quick responses, effective treatment and diagnoses
Hypothesis 3	AI, IoT, and smart technology increase the possibility of profiling subject health condition status with greater accuracy

As well as the statement beforehand, these hypotheses will be analysed within the bachelor thesis, trying to verify or falsify these approaches and give more specific insight into the thesis topic of Artificial Intelligence.

2.0 Methodology

In order to provide strong evidence for the bachelor thesis, a triangular approach as the research method was chosen. For this thesis, mainly qualitative scientific sources were used in order to understand the behaviour of the thesis phenomenon, as well as the evolution of AI Systems, interactions, or implementations. Therefore, books, as well as several online sources were chosen to analyse the hypothesis and statements made before.

Another focus within the content analysis was put on a handful of market reports from companies such as McKinsey and voicebot.ai, who conducted research over the past decades when AI first arose — creating the advantage of relying on long-term developments as well as social changes. These two non-empirical approaches offer the chance to focus on the "theoretical and general knowledge of science to classify its systematically" (Santoro, 2019, slide 5). In order to strengthen the secondary data, it was decided to implement case study approaches, including experiments & long-term studies conducted e.g., by MIT. To achieve the triangular approach, an empirical method was chosen: expert interviews that focus on the field of Health Care, AI and the implementation of such technology. That approach allowed deriving knowledge from actual experience rather than from theory or belief, as conducted in the scientific data. By choosing these three main methods, different perspectives are brought into the conducted research, looking at every angle of the subject of AI and its impact on the health sector and society's life. It is expected that these methods will either verify or falsify the thesis statement and hypotheses.

2.1 Literature Review

Primarily the thesis was build upon literature review. That is for the reason that literature review has the characteristic of "building research on and relating it to existing knowledge, building a block of all academic research activities, regardless of disciplines" (Snyder, 2019, p.333). According to Snyder, this approach makes literature review to a priority for all academic papers (ibid). Taking a closer look at the characteristics of literature review, it becomes clear that such methodology builds a "firm foundation for advancing knowledge and facilitating theory developments" (ibid). For these reasons, it was decided to include this approach as the primary source of research, gaining an overview of the area AI, mental health, smart cities, et cetera. As literature review can be reflected through a simple summary of sources or be organised through patterns and synthesis — new interpretation can arise ("Literature Reviews - The Writing, n.d.). These new levels give an opportunity for new interpretations and create an "excellent way of synthesising research findings to show the evidence on a meta-level". While this approach is defined as a quantitive approach rather than qualitative, the next methods are focused on a more specific level.

2.2 Case study

As a second source, it was decided to include case studies within the thesis — in order to include a qualitative research approach. This methodology is mostly used to "investigate and understand complex issues in real-world setting" (Harrison et al., 2017). In other words, "it analyses specific issues with boundaries of a specific environment, situation or organisation" ("Case Studies," n.d.). While case studies can be distinguished into three categories: explanatory case study, descriptive case study, and exploratory case study — this research paper only focuses on exploratory case studies (ibid). This form of case study "often is accompanied by additional data collection methods such as experiments". In this case, that definition reflects the approach in the bachelor thesis in form of e.g., conducted experiments from the MIT University (ibid). In order to include primary data within the methodology approach, the thesis includes a third research method. Therefore, the next subsection will deal with the introduction of expert interviews.

2.3 Expert Interviews

Focusing on expert interviews, primary data as a new approach is included — adding another method to the qualitative research approach (Hamill, 2014). In general, it can be defined as the oldest methodology approach, which consists of a conversation "between two people in which one person has the role of the researcher" (ibid). The probably most important characteristic of expert interviews is the fact that these are "carried out face-to-face, over telephone and internet or in a group setting" (ibid). One of its advantages is that the subject of the interview has no chance of non-response (Valenzuela & Shrivastava, n.d., p.12). Additionally, the high flexibility of personal expert interviews creates another advantage. That is for the reason that interviews can "vary from spontaneous too highly structured" scenarios (Hamill, 2014). While neither of these approaches meets the criteria that want to be met within these expert interviews — a semi structured/open-end approach was chosen. Including an aided interview guide with several questions that could help with the conversation, the interviewer has the advantage of being flexible and responsive throughout the interview (ibid). For the reason, that usually conversations can bring new insights — the sequence of questions can change and adapt to the newly learned/heard material. Therefore, it gives the interviewer the option to probe "more deeply into the initiated response" and getting an in-depth answer.

That flexibility and the empiric approach, are forming a new point of view and give new insights into the topic within the thesis — generating the approach to contribute to the overall statements and analysis. In order to dive into the thesis topic and understand the different areas AI can affect or be implemented, the following chapter will discuss and introduce the key theory definitions and explanations.

3.0 Key Theory Definitions & Explanations

During the last decade, technology has been evolving faster than ever witnessed before and with it society itself. For the reason that "technology never stands still", society and daily life have to evolve constantly as well (Woetzel et al., 2018, p.vi). According to Toffler, "We are the children of the next transformation" (Toffler, pp. 22 -23, 1980), focusing on the transformation into the technological age. Within this transformation, the digitalisation, several new terms, and new inventions arose, such as the Internet of Things (IoT), smart devices and artificial intelligence (AI), and smart cities. Especially at the beginning of the revolution, humans were suspicious about the usage of their private data for the reason that they have not grown up with these new inventions. With the younger generation of Millennials and Generation Z, who started growing up with mobile phones, computers and nowadays AI such as "Alexa", the suspicion to trust or not to trust companies with personal data stayed at an average of 80% in 2015 (Boston Consulting Group, 2016, slide 7). These numbers are still quite high and have to be reduced. Therefore, not only companies have to be more transparent about their data usage, but society has to change/adapt to these new technologies as well. Another downside arising as a consequence of new technologies is a high rate of mental illnesses such as anxiety and depression. According to Twenge et al., over the past ten years, the number for individuals suffering from mental health issues has more than doubled — especially within the younger generations, which would be triggered by technologies (2017). Even though these illnesses were negatively stimulated by technology in the first place — nowadays technology has the possibility to put a focus on these issues that affect the quality of life and improve it by up to "10-30%" (Woetzel, J., Remes, J., et al. 2018). For the reason that the thesis is built on four different key theory definitions and explanations — which will reoccur over and over again within the research paper — the following chapter will introduce the "Wave Approach by Toffler", three identities, neuroscience and lastly mental illnesses including depression, burn-out and anxiety.

3.1 The Wave Approach

As mentioned in the section before Toffler stated that "We are the children of the next transformation" (1980, pp. 22 -23). Nevertheless, what does he mean by that, and how can it be applied in our society today?

Looking back at former transformations / "Waves," it can be seen that Toffler has divided them into three categories, starting with the "First Wave, which unleashed 10.000 years ago" with the rise of agriculture (p. 25, 1980). This first wave took "thousands of years to play itself out" to manifest itself into society's daily life (Toffler, p.26, 1980). The Second Wave is the so-called industrial wave, which only took 300 years to be integrated into the routine of society (ibid). Back in 1980, Toffler defined the current wave/transformation as the "super industrial society". He explained that the "Third Wave" could not have a specific definition for the reason that it had no specific factor with deep "social upheaval and creative restructuring". Too many factors were included in the "Third Wave", such as the rise of the computers, the first Walkman, radio stations, and television providers. Even though Toffler decided not to specify on a specific name, he stated that the "Third Wave" will be more accelerative as the ones before (p. 26, 1980). According to Toffler, transformation and, therefore, "changes are not independent", meaning that society has to change as well in order for a transformation to work out (p.18, 1980). Therefore, the old assumptions from the previous wave have to be challenged. In this case, Toffler is focusing on the approach that a newly integrated code of behaviour and a clash of the new and old civilisation will form — creating a "fast emerging and evolving technology and lifestyle" (Toffler, p. 18, 1980).

When putting an eye on the older civilisation ("Second Wave"), most of them "do not think about the future and are sure that the world they know will last indefinitely" (Toffler, p.27, 1980). It is even said; they find it difficult even to imagine to form or adapt to a different way of life (ibid). Toffler states that the older generation within a transformational process recognises that "things are changing but assume that the change will pass by them and that nothing will shake their familiar economic framework" (ibid). Another theory the author is bringing to the theory is the assumption that the "Third Wave will sweep across history and complete itself in a few decades," bringing a "new way of life" (ibid). Focusing on the point that this assumption was made in 1980, the question

7

arises if our current transformation can still be seen as the "next transformation" from 1980 or if we are already within the next one. The collision of generations is forming again (Millennials and Generation Z vs. the older generations), which forms the theory that humanity is close to another transformation and therefore moving into the "Fourth Wave" — "The Ere of AI". Even though the author already mentioned machine intelligence within his book, the "Ere of AI" reaches another level by adding up small changes to form a transformation in regards to the perspective of life, society and thinking (Toffler, p.28, 1980) (Toffler, p.185, 1980). Moreover, we are right in front of it.

3.2 Identities of the Society

In order to understand on which level AI can interact with the human race and analyse the collected data, several components have to be taken into account. One of these components is the idea of three different identities every individual project on today's society and, therefore, on the AI.

As mentioned before in the previous section — through the Third Wave and the beginning Fourth Wave, many new technologies arrived and were implemented in modern society, changing the lifestyle of the human race in a revolutionary way. Part of this change was the rise of two new identities, additional to our real identity, which includes our real-life accomplishments and persona (Tansu, 2018). The first new identity which was introduced to our daily life is the so-called "Digital Identity" (ibid). It first emerged after Social Media was implemented in the day-to-day life of the human race (ibid). This identity can be described as everything an individual wants to show off on the social media platforms such as Instagram, Facebook, Snapchat, etc.. By posting pictures, statements or anything else — every individual who is using these platforms creates an image of themselves as they want to be perceived by others. The Third Identity, which is the most important for AI, is the "Digital Soul". The main characteristic of this approach is that every individual is not 100% aware of the third identity they create (ibid). It is evolving and building its knowledge every time an individual is using their location-based tools, their credit card, smartphones, and other systems that are connected to Google, Amazon, or similar platforms (ibid). As most consumers are not aware that they give away their data over these actions, applications, and devices, the "Digital Soul" creates probably the most accurate identity that reflects an individual on all levels (emotionally, socially, medically, etc.). The University of Ohio even states that AI probably knows our identity and emotional state better than your own family (Artificial Intelligence: The Insights You Need from Harvard Business Review, 2019, p. 137). Thus being said, a rough picture is created of how the three identities play an important role when interacting with AI — creating data, which will be explained further in the upcoming chapter 3.0 Artificial Intelligence and its impact on the quality of life.

3.3 Neuroscience

Within the last chapter, three identities were introduced in order to realise the impact of AI on the quality of life. However, to understand on which level these identities can be appealed too, an insight into neuroscience has to be given. Neuroscience gives insights into several processes of how we act, why, and with what emotions. This information can be identified and put into AI processing progresses, e.g., emotion detection in order to create a professional interaction with humans in certain emotional states or health conditions.

In general, neuroscience can be described as everything that focuses on the study of the nervous system, which includes the spinal cord, the brain itself, and all networks of the sensory nerves, called neurons (What is Neuroscience?, n.d.). The field integrates several disciplines and deals with knowledge about humans' thoughts, emotions, and behaviour (ibid). It opens up the possibility to understand the processes within the human brain (Cooper, n.d., p.1). For the reason that the brain has a quiet complex antonym consisting of several structural parts (Cronshaw, 2014). Mainly these parts can be distinguished and separated into two main areas. The Neocortex and the limbic system/ reptilian brain.

The Neocortex makes out up to 80% of the human brain. When focusing on its function, this part of the brain is mainly used to coordinate "higher-order thinking", such as using language or more in-depth problem-solving. Therefore, when it comes to decision making, the neocortex is the so-called rational part of the brain, which takes facts such as price and quality into account in order to come to a final choice (cognitive decision making). Even though every individual mostly thinks that their decisions are made consciously, the Limbic System focuses on emotional responsiveness and integration (Kolb and Wishaw, 2016, p. 398). These emotions, such as anger, fear, sadness, jealousy,

9

embarrassment, and joy, can operate outside "our immediate awareness"(ibid). Thus being said, it can be stated that arising subconscious emotions can overlap the rational decision making / rational preferences and change humans behaviour. Even though the Limbic System makes out such a small part of the brain, most processes within it are made emotionally or unconsciously (Lindstrom, 2008). According to Lindstrom, the emotions are the actors in which way our brains encode things of value (2008, p.26).

EMOTIONS

Happiness

Surprise

Anger

Disgust

Sadness

Fear

Fig.   *Combination of Emotions*, personal communication, 2018).

Focusing on Figure 1, it can be seen that all emotions can be categorised in two sections: in primary emotions and secondary combinations. While primary emotions are the ten standard feelings, the secondary combination are emotions that arise when primary emotions are combined. These combinations create then new emotions such as delight, guilt, hope, etc.. As mentioned before, emotions can occur out of an individual's consciousness. These unconscious emotions occur when an individual is not aware of the stimulus or "shift in their emotional state" (Lindstrom, 2008, p.76).

In general, it can be said that emotions are a response to a verbal or physiological appeal, which is "brief in duration" (ibid). Taking this into account, the human mind can be manipulated, appealed to on an emotional base, and driven into behaviour patterns, which also occur unconsciously up to 95% (Kuehn, 2013). Not only emotions alone create a way to trigger specific actions but also senses in combination with these emotions help to cause moods and responses. Lindstrom states that in order to fully engage the subject, it is more effective to connect a certain smell to the product, a sound to an approach, or even both, rather than relying on older techniques to "manipulate" emotions (2008, p.143). This approach can also be referred to as SensoryBranding (ibid).

An example of this SensoryBranding is the case study of Dunkin' Donuts in South Korea, who used the traffic on busses and sprayed the smell of coffee whenever their jingle came on the radio in order to increase sales in 2012 (Annear, 2012). About 350,000 citizens became part of this advertising approach of SensoryBranding while on their daily ride to work (ibid). At the end of this initiative, which lasted over several months, "the coffee company said that they saw a 16 percent spike in visitors at shops located by bus stops where vehicles were equipped with the smell-technology" (ibid). While at the same time, "coffee sales went up by 29 percent" (ibid). This example supports the SensoryBranding approach from Lindstrom, where emotions and, therefore, the behaviour is triggered subconsciously within the human's mind.

For the reason of the subconscious interference of emotions on individuals, different markets can profit from it. Nowadays, it is mostly used to manipulate society into buying consumer goods or other things in order to generate revenue in form of money, which is frown upon in society. Yet we are moving into the next wave the "Era of AI", where technologies open up so many more opportunities to interfere in a less unethical manner, e.g., within the Health Sector, helping, adapting, and preventing illnesses.

3.4 The Correlation between Depression, Anxiety and Burn-out

When focusing on illnesses that can be diagnosed easily or the therapy can be adapted, most of the time, people think of a rash, Parkinson, etc., basically everything that is visually visible to the human eye. But what about all the silent illnesses, such as depression and anxiety (Powers, n.d.)? For the reason that these three illnesses are the most common ones to arise in today's society and the focus of the three hypotheses rely on depression, anxiety and burn-out — this chapter aims to analyse such diseases.
All individuals who suffer from depression, burn-out, anxiety have to reach out for help by themselves, which means first of all being diagnosed with these issues and secondly being treated within therapy or taking medication. For the reason that most of the time,

subjects with such disorders shy away and do not make the first step to getting diagnosed because they are not motivated - new solutions have to be found (Powers, n.d.). Focusing on this problem, the National Institute of Mental Health indicates "that 37% adults" with these sicknesses do not even receive any diagnoses or treatment — mostly for the reason of health care systems (Powers, n.d.). This issue of not being diagnosed and no capabilities for treatments opens up another huge concern in regards to higher suicide rates, less productivity, etc.. When putting the focus of attention on these mental sicknesses in the U.S. — were depression, burn-out and anxiety are a massive issue — it becomes clear that around 43.8 million Americans suffer from at least one of these diseases (Mental Health By the Numbers | NAMI: National Alliance on Mental Illness, n.d.). The NAMI states that every fifth adult is suffering from a mental illness in one year, which means that these illnesses can reoccur, or an individual has been suffering for many years. For this reason, that every year the number of affected individuals is growing, the demand for therapy, doctors, etc. is rising from day to day.

In the following paragraphs, the terms will be explained to understand the connection between these three illnesses. In general, it can be stated that some people are more predisposed to mental issues than others (Powers, n.d.). According to Powers, these conditions can affect any individual at some point in life (ibid). Concentrating on the mental issue of depression, the disease can be defined as the most common disorders in the U.S., with approximately 16.2 Million people suffering from it (ibid). As depression counts to mental illnesses, it has an effect on the human mind. Nevertheless, the condition can be "accompanied by physical symptoms such as fatigue, inability to focus or perform tasks that were easy before" (ibid). Doctors talk about a major depression or depression episode whenever an individual shows these symptoms, including debilitating sadness for weeks, months, or even years (Hanai et al., 2018 p.1716).

Not only depression intervenes with the subjects' life, but also anxiety and burn-out play an essential role in the spectrum of mental illnesses. Anxiety can be characterised on an emotional base, such as "feelings on tension, worried thoughts and physical change" (McFadden, 2019). Not only that the individual usually has recurring intrusive thoughts or concerns, but these characteristics can lead to avoiding certain situations mainly out of worry (ibid). Part of the physical change, which can be visible to others are, for example, "sweating, tumbling, dizziness or rapid heart rate" (ibid). One common trigger of anxiety are "transition periods and moments of change"(Abbas, 2019). Anxiety leads the human body to have arising emotions of, e.g., stress, which is forming into anxiety. In order to understand anxiety on different levels, it has to be distinguished in two different types (Koutsimani et al., 2019). Primary trait anxiety, which is defined as the degree an individual perceives stressful situations or its level of threat (Spielberger, 1966). Secondly, the state anxiety. It can be described as every reaction of an individual towards a situation after "having appraised it as threatening" (ibid).

With similar symptoms, the illness of burnout arises. Burnout can be described as a psychological syndrome, similar to the illnesses of depression and anxiety introduced before (Koutsimani et al., 2019). It can be identified by its symptoms of "emotional exhaustion, feelings of cynicism and reduced personal accomplishments" (ibid). When working too hard or being constantly under stressful conditions at work or even within the private life, burnout can be triggered in each individual's mindset/brain (ibid).

When focusing on these three mental illnesses, a few correlations can be seen, e.g., the trigger, the symptoms, or the characteristics. Over the past decades' several scientists and doctors were asking themselves if all three mental illnesses are the same, only overlap on some stages or build each other up to the next level, e.g., anxiety leads sooner or later to depression (ibid).

While an occurring burnout hardly depends on the personality and external factors an individual can stand against, depression and anxiety relate to the personality itself (ibid). Even though these issues arise on different levels, an overlap between depression and burnout can be seen (ibid). According to Freudenberg, "people who suffer from burnout look and act as if they were depressed" (1974). Therefore, they show the same physical characteristics such as loss of interest or pleasure, fatigue, and loss of energy (ibid). According to Koutsimani et al. — the researchers, Bianchi et al., also stand behind the idea of a correlation between depression and anxiety in an emotional state (2019). On the other hand, some studies focus on the differences between those illnesses. While depression is context-free, burnout is work-related (ibid) - still, the symptoms are similar and therefore overlap on some parts. Focusing on the correlation of anxiety and burnout, it can be clearly said that these illnesses are connected/related. According to Cole, anxiety

13

acts as a protective factor against all threatening situations an individual interprets as alarming (2014).

This approach, as well as the two defined anxieties (trait & state), focus on the personality and its limits of accepting certain situations, which collides with the focus of the burnout - what level of stress a particular individual can stand against in its daily life. Therefore, it can be stated that burnout and anxiety are interrelated and correlate on several levels. Similar to the collusion of depression and anxiety. They do not correlate on several levels, but they show the same symptoms. As it can be seen, all illnesses are correlating on several levels. When thinking about triggers for such illnesses, hypothesis 1 comes back to mind: "New technologies originally created the issue of anxiety, burn-out, and depression but now has the potential to create solutions.".

In general, it can be stated that technology made "our lives inexorably more efficient and easier compared to past generations" (McFadden, 2019). It allowed humanity to focus on more important tasks (ibid). Nevertheless, some studies show that several technologies "making us less happy" (ibid). An example for that are computers. If these are used over hours and hours a day (such as, e.g., at work), they will increase the probability of depression (ibid). Another factor is the internet, with all its information. The reason why it could have such a massive impact on the humans' mind is that the brain is "not laid out to be bathed in so much information all the time" (ibid). As the brain can adapt to a certain amount of data and information, an overload changes the behaviour, e.g., individuals start "feeling that the real-life is boring and slow" compared to the internet with continuous stimuli (ibid). This so-called "popcorn brain" can lead to "serious mental health issues," such as anxiety (Fear of missing out), and depression (ibid). However, the probably most interruptive technology that had an impact on our life, on a positive but also negative sense, is the smartphone. For the reason that the smartphone is widely adapted in our society and humanity always carries these with them, a separation anxiety forms (ibid). The smartphone does not only trigger anxiety but also the possibility for an individual to be contacted 24/7 around the world. This reachability can lead to worsening anxiety disorder and burnout syndrome (ibid). Thus being said, technology and its impact can be defined as a double-edged sword. Without a doubt, it can trigger certain sicknesses such as depression, anxiety, and burnout, but only if those are used excessively. For this reason, the first statement of hypothesis 1 that technology triggers such illnesses could be supported.

Yes, technology can have a negative impact on individuals, but can it also create solutions by diagnosing or better the situation with mental health issues as suggested by hypothesis 1 and 2? In order to understand today's technologies impact on nowadays life, the next chapter will explain arising new technologies such as Artificial Intelligence (AI) and the small processes behind it.

4.0 The Technology behind Artificial Intelligence

Currently, a significant amount of research is focusing on the potentialities of Artificial Intelligence (AI). It could be even stated that this is the next significant paradigm shift for humanity after the last great invention of the mobile phone and, therefore, the "Ere of AI". In order to understand how AI can impact the health sector several aspects and the technology behind it have to be understood.

Today AI already has the possibility to improve certain aspects of humans' lives, such as work, driving cars, or just our smartphone, which are highly implemented and accepted in our society (Eadicicco, 2019). Nearly every household has at least one AI in their home, e.g., Alexa, Google Home, Netflix, or just even Siri or the Google Assistant (ibid). AI will not only make the world more efficient and more effective for individuals, but it will also improve the quality of life on many levels (ibid). Even though humans use these technologies in their daily life to enhance their lifestyle or just to have more fun, the process behind the AI seems to be a mystery. In general, AI can be defined as a collection of similar technologies, which a computer can use in order to make data-based and humanlike decisions (ibid). For the AI to understand and process this data, several small processes are implemented before they can interact with other machines or individuals. For humans to understand these interactions, the history of AI, as well as several terms, have to be explained.

After the term of Artificial Intelligence arose first in 1956 on the Campus Dartmouth College, it was perceived differently "as its actually being put to use" nowadays, and it is still evolving (Pathak & Bhandari, 2018, pp. 3 - 5). The definition of AI back in the days was described as "every aspect of learning or any other feature of intelligence which can be so precisely described that a machine can be made to simulate it" (Pathak & Bhandari, 2018, p.5). For the reason that this "basic concept of AI has not changed in a wider sense," the evolvement focuses on its application and new layers (Pathak & Bhandari, 2018, p.3). Therefore, AI can be described as a machine learning process in today's society. These robotic systems are understood as a programming paradigm, "where the engineer provides examples comprising what the expected output of the program should be, given the input" (Taulli, n.d.). Machine Learning (ML) systems then take all the information into account to explore a variety of possible outcomes (ibid). According to Chanchaichujit et al., ML is the core part of AI, dealing with the simulation of intelligent behaviour in computers (2019, p.64). It allows the AI to mimic human behaviour, which led the machine to learn and accumulate information and solve problems (ibid). Through all the given inputs by interactions or programming, the AI has the possibility to find and learn an individual's pattern and learn even further to "classify and use regression to determine a suitable output" (ibid). Pattern recognition, in this case, is an essential characteristic of such processes. As ML enables the AI to learn an individual's "normal behaviour" pattern, it is to detect abnormalities by comparing newly collected data with the learned pattern model (Brugnara et al., n.d.).

Consequently, ML within the AI brings the prospect to establish correlations between already collected data, making suggestions, which gives the human race a massive advantage in several sectors (Chanchaichujit et al., 2019, p.64). To adapt to an even higher level, the algorithms of AI have to be taken into account. Algorithms, in general, are a "series of computations from the most simple and most complex areas" (Taulli, n.d.). When focusing on ML, algorithms are being used to "process data and encode them in a model which can be used to make predictions on new data" (ibid). Machine Learning uses the regression of the algorithms in order to improve its interactions and predictions on a regular basis (Chanchaichujit et al., 2019, p.65). As mentioned in the previous sector, the load of information through the internet (digital information) are increasing, so the implementation of AI can help with the amount of data even more efficient than humans since the machines are not dedicated to illnesses such as "popcorn brain" (ibid). Therefore, ML primary aims "to allow machines itself to understand information without human intervention" (ibid).

Another vital characteristic to understand the importance and capabilities of AI are its "Neural Networks" (Taulli, n.d.). The neural networks have many connections within each AI, mimicking the structure of a human brain — creating the capacity to "summarise complex information into simple, tangible results (ibid). Neural Networks allow AI to be trained and construct to learning processes (ibid). Therefore, the next step for AI after ML is the implementation of Neuro Learning (NL) (Chanchaichujit et al., 2019, p.65). Two different approaches of learning arise within the machine learning: supervised and unsupervised. These approaches create unseen errors for the reason of unseen sequences "of input events," only focusing on specific areas (ibid). NL uses this basic approach of machine learning, concentrating on the two ideas, connecting it to neural networks, which again create algorithms that work similarly "to the human brain" (ibid). The unique quality NL brings to the bigger picture is that it can "extract information more efficiently, the more it learns" (ibid). In addition, NL brings the characteristic to sense and notice if the information is wrong, which gives the AI space to adapt on a new level and mimic humans' communication and processes (ibid). While earlier systems were able to read pure implemented data, through Neuro Systems, the algorithms today are "better suited to analyse disordered and complicated data" (Chanchaichujit et al., 2019, p.66).

Through the approach of NL, the integrated system of deep learning (DL) can be introduced. This system is used in order to analyse all the data which was captured through ML & NL (ibid). In general, it can be viewed as a "generalisation of classical pattern recognition" either of the environment or individual systems or subjects (Pedrycz & Shyi-Ming, 2018, p. 3). DL creates the capacity for AI systems to predict outcomes, using the collected & analysed data (Chanchaichujit et al., 2019, p.66). While NL creates the decision-making process of an AI accurate, DL processes "break down all layers within the Neuro Learning and lead them towards the Machine Learning Systems" in order to get better outcomes (ibid).

Through all this information collected by the different learning layers, the AI creates a decision-making function (ibid). The DL process "begins by going through the Machine Learning process", starting to transform the binary data "into multi-layer processes with neural networks" (ibid). All information/ data that make it through this layer are classified into predicted outcomes of the DL processes, which are the responses individuals get from AI nowadays when, e.g., asking them to order food, making a call, or predicting car accidents (ibid).

Therefore, the statement can be made that these three learning systems led the AI to its capability to answer our questions, predict certain situations, and intervene in our life within certain aspects.

4.1 The Internet of Things

With all the data, AI is producing, analysing, collecting, and recognising one aspect plays an important role: The Internet of Things (IoT). The term of IoT first came up back in the 80s (Pathak & Bhandari, 2018, p. 26). Primary in the early 2000s, the phrase started being mentioned in "scientific journals, conferences, and magazines" (ibid). It was not until 2009, only 11 years ago, that IoT officially was recognised after the number of devices that were connected to the internet exceeded the number of living people on earth (ibid). It was alone in 2014 the IoT started gaining recognition all over the industries (ibid). Thus being said, it can be seen that IoT is quite new to the world, connecting it to AI and giving it the possibility to communicate/exist in our world (ibid). Therefore the statement can be made that IoT "works all around us" (Woetzel et al., 2018, p.24).

Taking a step back, the internet was initially invented to connect two computers — "sitting in two different parts of the world" — with each other (Pathak & Bhandari, 2018, p.6). While most individuals connect the term internet with the association www. (web), it has to be defined as two separate things (ibid). The web can be described as a "pet of the internet," meaning certain other aspects create the internet itself (ibid). According to Chanchaichujit et al., the internet allowed us to advance on a technical basis and impacted our style of living on the level of communication systems as well as data-sharing systems (2019, p.3). Looking back at the original task of the internet, nowadays several new technologies were introduced that are connected with it. This includes technologies such as smartphones, tablets, Smart TVs, Smart Watches, Smart Fridges, AI in general, etc., supporting the statement from Pathak & Bandari mentioned before. A high number of devices joined the internet over the past decade. Till today five billion of "non-computer items" are implemented in the immense network of the internet (Pathak & Bhandari, 2018, p.12) (Woetzel et al., 2018, p.23). This number will grow drastically within the next year connecting up to 20.4 Billion smart devices (Woetzel et al., 2018, p.24). All these gadgets are defined as things, which then build the wide world of the "Internet of Things" (IoT). Woetzel et al. state that by this year (2020), 6.1 Billion mobile phone users will be connected to the internet, which shows a constant growing the IoT network (Woetzel et al., 2018, p.23).

Within this context, the IoT can be described as the "global network of "smart" versions of regular physical objects" (Pathak & Bhandari, 2018, p.12). In the context of the IoT and today's society, smart objects are everything that is able to connect to the internet — creating new possibilities for these objects to offer applications and evolve (ibid). This does not mean that all IoT devices have to be connected to the internet all the time to identify as such (Pathak & Bhandari, 2018, p. 36). They can "operate offline most of the time and only connect to the internet" in order to update the data with the Cloud (ibid). Most of the time, these objects of IoT are used for data collection, which are gathered by its implemented sensors for measuring specific parameters such as, e.g., the heart rate through smartwatches (Pathak & Bhandari, 2018, p.14). These data pieces are then stored within the device and saved in the cloud later on for further analysis within the AI itself or other AI circles — generating meaningful information about individuals, reflecting their third identity, which they not aware of (Chapter 2.3) (ibid). An important characteristic of IoT devices is not only their daily task of collecting and analysing data but also the ability to communicate with each other, giving them new opportunities to learn, develop new knowledge and understand patterns (Aher, 2018).

As these definitions describe all IoT devices, a distinction can be made between customer IoT and industrial IoT (Pathak & Bhandari, 2018, p.28). The customer IoT consists of already developed devices, which are ready for consumption by each individual. These devices are connected to each other, e.g.; smartphones are connected to a watch or another smartphone — or to other local networks via, e.g., Bluetooth or the WiFi (ibid). On the other hand, the industrial IoT exists in today's society, which includes all devices that are "custom-made for specific enterprises and industrial scenarios," e.g., within the government (ibid). These devices are then only connected directly to the internet and not to other smart devices or networks (ibid).

Taking all these information into account, it can be declared that IoT can be summarised as a tool that "facilitated the exchange and access to real-time data from any place in the world at any given time", promoting its environment "where individuals can be connected to the web services provided by such technologies" (IoT devices, e.g., AI) (Chanchaichujit et al., 2019, p.3).

These services and the constant access to the internet and other IoT services can be provided in so-called smart cities, which will be taken into account in the next subchapter, giving insights into the evolvement of smart cities and their possibilities when introduced to society.

4.2 The Rise of Smart Cities and its Impact on Human Life

Over the last decades, cities got smarter and smarter, meaning more livable and more responsive (Woetzel et al., 2018, p. v). Even though humanity evolved immensely in regards to technology — today reflects only a preview of what technology can do and will do in the future (ibid). For the reason that technology is no longer a constraint in the present and future society, humanity had the opportunity to make "rapid advances such as IoT, machine learning" etc. which paved the way for them to evolve and create innovations (Woetzel et al., 2018, p.21). As mentioned before, inventions and change are moving faster than ever before, expanding in ways humanity previously never imagined. Looking for example at the invention of smartphones, it becomes clear that through its widespread use and acceptance in society the smartphones become the key of today's smart cities (Woetzel et al., 2018, p.1). The advantage of smartphones is that a wide range of society is able to use them (Woetzel et al., 2018, p.21). With one tap, several information, vital services, etc. are available for the consumer (ibid). For that reason that smartphones have the opportunity to deliver instant information about several aspects such as transit, traffic, safety alerts, payment methods, and health services, the smartphone becomes part of AI systems (Woetzel et al., 2018, p.1). Therefore, it has the opportunity to deliver information and transfer a "river of information" to the government, companies, etc. for further analysis and pattern recognition in order to predict outcomes (Woetzel et al., 2018, p.23). Mostly this data is collected by the layers of sensors (voice, heart rate) on the smartphone and other devices — taking in every aspect of their physical environment (ibid).

20

When talking about smart cities, individuals mostly think about all technologies that are implemented within it. However, the statement of "smart" also indicates the use of technology and the use of its collected data (ibid). Thus being said, "smart" in the context of cities should be implemented "to make better decisions and deliver" a better standard of life which can be reached by the usage/implementation of technology as well as the aspects mentioned above (ibid). Smartness, in this case, is simply just a tool to help the cities improving living standards and serve the citizens (Woetzel et al., 2018, p. 33). By collecting different real-time data from all smart devices such as phones, smartwatches, etc., the city can become more and more comprehensive (Woetzel et al., 2018, p.23). The city can, for example, watch "events as they unfold" and use this information to understand how "demand patterns change," which gives the city and other individuals the possibility to react to it faster at lower costs (ibid). Nevertheless, "smart" can not only be defined on this level but on three different layers.

1. The Technology Layer

This layer is defined as the "critical masses of smartphones and other sensors," which are connected by high-speed networks, allowing the communication between individuals and devices itself (Woetzel et al., 2018, p.2). The sensors within the devices then have the ability to take constant readings of different variables such as traffic via GPS, energy consumption, heart rate, air consumption (ibid).

2. The Specific Application Layer

The Layer of Specific Applications concentrates on the task of translating raw data into alerts, insights, preventions, etc., which can be or are already introduced into sectors such as security, health, and community (ibid).

3. The Public Usage Layer

The third and last layer focuses on the implementation of applications within the society (ibid). It states that applications are only successful if widely used by society and managed to change individuals behaviour (ibid). This includes the transparency of applications in order for humans to make better choices in their daily life (ibid).

In order to complete the operation of all smart applications — companies and residents play an essential and active role in shaping the "city's performance" (ibid). Hence to the ever-growing human race, which is drawn to cities because of better jobs and perspectives — cities nowadays face a lot of pressure (ibid). With the "Era of AI" and other new technologies, the cities have a new set of tools, and a new gained digital intelligence, which can help with the information flow and improvements in daily life. With all-new technologies, it can even be stated that the relationship between the government and the citizens they serve changes (Woetzel et al., 2018, p.15). The cities can use this insight and the technology within it to take the "pulse of the public opinion on a wide range of issues" (ibid). Nevertheless, in order for them to focus on issues such as Health Care (HC), more of the population has to be online (ibid). This task of bringing more people online should be perceived as priority No. 1. That is for the reason that without humans being connected, no information would be generated, and no analysis could be taken place within devices. Consequently, no input for the AI would be generated, excluding the possibility of improving daily life. Therefore, the goal of every smart city should focus on public services such as free WiFi and a general cheaper distribution of smartphones on the companies' site in order to begin the improvement of the quality of life/living standards.

When taking all this information about smart cities into account, their image from Sci-Fi movies with flying cars, hoverboards, etc. have to be redefined. By using the information gathered and including "an overlay of intelligence," the city can not only expand on capacity within the city walls but also on the lifespan of existing assets as for example elderly care, health care, pollution (Woetzel et al., 2018, p.22). Therefore, the perceived image of smart cities has to be reconsidered and newly introduced as a "places where different actors amply technology and data to make better decisions and achieve a better quality of life" (ibid).

However, what exactly is meant by the quality of life?
Concentrating on its definition, many dimensions have to be taken into account (Woetzel et al., 2018, p.2). This includes, for example, if the citizens feel safe if they can breathe the air without a health hazard if health services are provided in every city district, etc. (ibid). According to the MGI, gathered data in smart cities could improve the quality of life in regards to health, time, and convenience (Woetzel et al., 2018, p.4 & p.33). That indicates about 10 – 30 % of all indicators that have an impact on societies' daily life can be improved (ibid). In order to collect and make use of important data, several devices have to be implemented in society to deliver data that improves their lives. Therefore, a

significant focus has to rely on smart devices and data collection within the cities, which will be reflected in the following section.

4.3 Smart Devices as AI & Data Collection

Humanity nowadays uses smart devices on a daily basis, but most of the time, the subjects cannot define what exactly these devices are compromised of and what they are able to do with all the data they collect.

In general smart devices are all objects that can interact with human beings, analyse data, run through learning processes by themselves, and recognise a pattern. Therefore smart devices are an Artificial Intelligence device that brings several inventions and possibilities into society and smart cities. Nevertheless, before scientists, as well as society itself, decided to implement AI and, therefore, smart devices in today's manner, it started off with the idea to build "human-like robots that could understand us" (Pathak & Bhandari, 2018, p. 6). In some aspects, precisely this happened - AI understands us and exceeds expectations by learning and predicting specific outcomes. Therefore, nowadays, our society and especially cities can be described as virtual market places, which have an impact on the influence of connections in the physical world - meaning people, products, machines, and systems. All these factors form one virtual world, which can be analysed by Artificial Intelligences (Chanchaichujit et al., 2019, p.3). For smart devices/AI to track and collect this data and form the market place we expect, sensors are being used to take in all information. These sensors distracted information from the environment the device is interacting with, e.g., microphones, measurement of heart rate. Thus being said, sensors can be generalised as "small electronic components designed to sense/detect a specific parameter" — sound, temperature, etc. (ibid). Through these sensors, the devices have the ability to "continuously record and store data in devices" (Pathak & Bhandari, 2018, p.14). According to Pathak & Bhandari, the sensors are the core element of all AI devices — besides ML, NL, and DL — for the reason that otherwise, no data would be collected and generated (2019, p.29). When a sensor comes to action, the physical phenomenon they measure formed into electoral signals, e.g., microphones are converting sound vibration into a signal for the device, which can be analysed (ibid).

When focusing on current trends within the industry of Artificial Intelligences, the most popular and probably also the most common object adapted and accepted in society are voice recognition systems such as Alexa, Siri, Google Home, Google Assistant, etc. (Eadicicco, 2019). They are not only the most common AI devices used in a human's normal life, but it is also the most advanced device in this sector (Artificial Intelligence: The Insights You Need from Harvard Business Review, 2019, p.6). These voice assistant devices hit the market in 2017 with a rising popularity "out spacing predictions" (Kinsella, 2018a). According to Kinsella, smart speaker technology has "grown faster than any other consumer technology" — even faster than mobile phones (2018a). Not only with its fast implementation in the market of AI but also with its endless possibilities to be integrated and used, gave the technology a push in sales (ibid). The Harvard Business Review even states that voice recognition systems are equal to human performances/interactions — reflecting the newly implemented technologies of AI (ML, NL and DL) (Artificial Intelligence: The Insights You Need from Harvard Business Review, 2019, p. 8). According to Kinsella, the shipments of such smart speakers/assistants rose up to 35 % in the whole world (Kinsella, 2019a). Meaning a whole of 92 Million smart assistants are placed in homes, apartments, and other facilities - collecting data, analysing it, and getting a picture of every individual living there (ibid).

Even though the sales growth of smart speakers slew down in 2019, sales will still "continue to grow quickly" (ibid). The volume though "will be suppressed due to the substitute effect of voice assistants and its access" to coming and already existing applications (ibid). The more smart speakers are adapted and implemented in society /households; more and more consumers will buy more voice assistants, which they can access in their home (ibid). The probably most important technology introduced within smart assistant devices, which made it possible for them to interact with human beings are the natural language processing processes (NLP). With the NLP, several aspects are brought together to achieve the maximum in the technology of voice recognition. This includes AI, computer science, and linguistic (Taulli, n.d.). All these technologies are focusing together on the goal of teaching machines to understand and process human language (ibid). For the reason that the language of humans has evolved and changed over the previous millennia, challenges for the NLP System arise (ibid). Therefore, the system has to focus on different levels of dexterity, precision, and discernment in order to form into a fully functional voice recognition system. Nevertheless, NLP has "entered a thrilling period of new possibilities" (ibid). NLP brings not only the opportunity for voice recognition systems to analyse the language of individuals but also to build tools that can engage with "a level of expressive intricacy," which was not imaginable just a decade ago (ibid). Even though the technology of smart assistants evolved immensely over the past three years at a fast pace, no other invention ever developed before, it still is in a time transition, and several players of the economic system are investing in multiple layers in this technology (Kinsella, 2018a).

A massive transition of voice recognition systems is the advancement in the emotional reading of an individual using the device. Just recently, Amazon filed for a patent to detect users' illnesses and the emotional state (Kinsella, 2018b). They state that through this patent Alexa and all other voice assistants from Amazon will be able to identify emotional conditions through the interaction with the voice recognition systems (ibid). In this case, Alexa or Echo would use data "to personalise user interaction and offer" help, medicine, or other products and services (ibid). With the option of physical and emotional detection Amazons voice recognition systems can be modified in regards to reactions, requests, and suggestions that are made by the user (ibid). Certain embodiments may even be determined with one or more physical or seminal characteristics — which can be used on the users' voice input e.g., an excited seminal state or sad emotional state (ibid). Thus being said, the voice recognition systems have two learn from previous interactions to determine the physical and emotional characteristics of the user — so "highly relevant content for" the interaction can be picked— creation high relevancy in the future of voice recognition systems (ibid). Another advantage arising with the recognition of emotional and physical detection is the improvement of the interaction with Alexa or similar systems (ibid). It gives the device the advantage to appear more humanlike by analysing these newly detected information and interpreted them due to the cues extracted from human speech (ibid). The reason why the emotional state can be analysed through a voice recognition system such as Alexa lies in the various information language or speech carries in them (Polzin & Waibel, n.d., p.1). The human language itself has several cues within its acoustic levels that can give information about the users' emotional state (ibid). To give voice assistants the possibility to sense the emotional state of the speaker within a dialogue or interaction with the assistant itself is crucial for several reasons (ibid). Depending on the emotional state, the true meaning of a sentence, and its words can be analysed (ibid). For example, looking only at the said words, the meaning differs when also taking in the emotions or the emotional state within this conversation/sentence (ibid). Therefore, several emotional dimensions have to be taken into account. This includes, for example, the emotional attitude of the speaker towards the hearer - which can also be the AI of voice recognition (ibid). Another important detail that has to be taken into the analysis of the emotional state is the emotional attitude towards responses or messages received by the assistant or even another human being (ibid). The choice of words as well as the acoustic articulation of the speakers' interaction give insights to their emotional state (ibid). Although using this system of voice recognition to identify the emotional state is an easy way to integrate preventive methods in daily life, the combination of different systems improves the accuracy of correct interpretations and analysis of emotions. Therefore, the system of face recognition will be introduced.

While the voice recognition systems manly focus on cues within the speech of the subject (voice pitch or intensity), face recognition systems rely mostly on the face (expression, eye movements, etc.) (Emotion-modulated attention improves expression recognition: A deep learning model, 2017). In the case of facial recognition, certain features within the face give specific information about the emotional state e.g., the eyes can reflect fear as well as joy depending on the expansion of the iris (Wegrzyn et al., 2017, p.2). At the same time, the mouth mainly can show happiness due to smiling or other movements with the lips (ibid). Similar to the voice recognition systems, only specific cues can be identified to show the emotional state of the user. However, when combining both systems — voice recognition and facial recognition — better results can be achieved (Akrouf et al., 2011, p. 230). One significant advantage with these biometric systems is their high acceptance in society for the reason that these are already implemented in our smartphones, e.g., unlocking the phone (ibid). As mentioned before, both systems are focusing on different biometric traits, which gives them more reliability as well as data security when combined (ibid). Through the approach of AI to use collected information through the environment and interaction with individuals to analyse emotions — it creates a massive advantage for the health sector in regards to mental illness, which are mostly diagnosed on an emotional level. According to the landmark study of the University of Ohio -- Artificial Intelligences and their algorithms are now "better at detecting emotions than people are" as well as they are more advanced in interpreting, processing and also simulating human emotions (Artificial Intelligence: The Insights You Need from Harvard Business Review, 2019, p. 137). In order to understand the impact of the machines process of analysing and interpreting emotions, forming their outcomes more precisely than humans, Chapter 5.0 will focus on its implementations within the health sector and other AI devices that help diagnosing such illnesses mentioned previously.

Studying the previously collected knowledge, it is definite that at all gathered data w from emotional and physical detection become part of the Digital Soul. This means that the user is not really aware of which information they give away. Additionally, these newly detected information can be combined with the user age, demographics, browser history, etc. in order to create a clear picture of an individual's living standards, struggles, and interests, improving certain aspects within HC such as diagnosis or treatment.

When focusing on the fact that all data will be collected from individuals who will give up their private data, primary privacy issues arise. Additionally, other challenges emerge when AI is implemented in smart cities, future smart cities, and our daily life. In order to reflect on these issues, subsection 4.6 will consider and analyse such impressions to review certain obstacles that have to be overcome for AI devices being implemented in a broader spectrum.

4.4 Challenges of AI and its Implementation in Smart Cities

With new technologies, not only opportunities emerge within society. Additionally, obstacles/challenges arise that have to be overcome in order for AI to have a positive impact. These challenges do not only focus on earning trust but also on the implementation of such technologies

As with the integration of other technologies before, humanity again is skeptical of nowadays implementation of AI. Especially with the ever-arising mistrust of the misuse of data, which will be collected with such technology. Therefore, the data privacy terms have to be investigated, and certain issues within it have to be addressed (Lim et al., 2018, p.93). In order to overcome the mistrust in data privacy companies and government agencies have to create a "valid and sustainable value for citizens and visitors" (ibid). In this case, not only the issue of the misuse of data plays an important role, but also the potential monitoring with smart devices could hinder individuals from interacting with such tools (Car, n.d.). Therefore, governments and companies selling these devices have to promise no harm to individuals, which means that the collected personalised data will only be used to match the subjects' personal preferences in sectors such as health (ibid).

Coming back to the issue of mistrust in the technology and the use of data, this obstacle can be seen as the "biggest reservation people have, when it comes to sharing personalised data" (ibid). Society has the fear that their data is going to be used against them (ibid). To earn the trust of such skeptics, the use of data has to be communicated on a transparent level — through governments and providing companies (ibid). An example of perfectly earned trust are the companies of Apple and Uber (ibid). These companies managed to communicate their strategies and use of data transparently, which earned them the trust of their customers, who willingly handed over their credit card information when using the services (ibid). For the reason that transparency succeeds when it comes to data privacy and earning trust in society, AI distributors should focus on these factors to open new markets and have the possibility to operate on a wider range. They also should communicate their commitment and communicate their approach and prepare themselves for imperfections — just for the reason that this technology is relatively new to the world and still needs improvement on some levels (ibid). Therefore, for AI to work in cities/smart cities, private life, and society itself, companies and governments have to listen to the feedback of citizens and visitors to improve continuously (ibid). This approach also has to be communicated towards humanity for the reason that their feedback and their data will contribute to the greater good/improvement of the quality of life (ibid).

While these challenges mentioned above mainly focus on the perception of society towards AI, the following issues focus on the technology and implementation itself. As AI describes a wide field of smart devices such as smartwatches, glasses, voice recognition, and facial recognition systems, etc. the collected information and sources have to be integrated and have to interact with each other (Lim et al., 2018, p.93). To achieve a high level of knowledge and qualitative information to analyse interactions, recognise patterns, etc. these different types of data have to be connected (ibid). Even though the approach to connect all these devices data could be difficult because of its different structures — with efforts and high focus of companies offering these technologies, this goal can be achieved (ibid). This interconnection opens up new possibilities to analyse and combine collected information and data to improve the knowledge and the interaction of devices and humanity (ibid).

Even though companies and governments could try everything to protect an individual's data with software etc. every time a subject connects their smart devices to the internet, the risk of being hacked rises (Chanchaichujit et al., 2019, p. 24). With more and more devices being connected a barrier breaks for data transmission (ibid). As a result of this break, conditions for cyber-attacks are created (ibid). For the reason that this threat gives more concerns in regards to privacy — secure mechanisms are required and have to be implemented within the systems of the IoT itself (ibid). One solution to overcome this challenge of higher cyber risks are blockchains (Pathak & Bhandari, 2018, p.16). These blockchains are tools that are full of entries that are shared with a group of other devices. This approach of a group that connects all its devices reflects the idea of IoT and, therefore, can be implemented in the case of securing the system from cyber-attacks (ibid). That is for the reason that blockchains bring the ability to encrypt data and need verification to ensure that it is stored correctly (ibid). However, the characteristic which makes blockchains unique is that entries and data once uploaded/stored within it cannot be tampered with (ibid). In other terms, the blockchain can be described as a "decentralised network" with no central authority (ibid). This means everybody has the same information without any distortions of this data (Pathak & Bhandari, 2018, p.18). Mainly when focusing on the use of AI in the health sector, these preventive actions to hinder cyber-attacks is highly crucial for its implementation on a wider spectrum within daily life.

For this reason, the next chapter will focus on possible improvements by AI technologies as well as their impact on individuals suffering from mental health conditions.

5.0 AI in Smart Cities with the Focus on Health

For the reason that Europe and especially Germany have many restrictions in regards to data transferring and high data privacy laws, the focus for this section will rely on America. In regards to already introduced AI technologies and future approaches within the health market, America has not only advanced their approaches but also lowered its barrier of data privacy. Another reason why America portrays the perfect market is their low offers of health care solutions for society. With AI as a new approach, some obstacles within the American market can be overcome. North American cities, for example, already implemented AI in the health sector and tend to lead the market, which gives America as a country the advantage of knowledge (Woetzel et al., 2018, p. 11). Not only the knowledge of what technologies will do to help adapting the health sector market but also how individuals react to such technologies within their lives.

Focusing on the health sector, Woetzel et al. state that today's smart technologies/ AI are able to "accelerate emergency response time by 20 - 35 %," which will reduce fatalities by 8 - 10% (Woetzel et al., 2018, p.35). Nowadays, subjects can reach limits when faced with an emergency, and the ability to make one phone call fails because of e.g., injuries. Therefore, responding effectively to emergencies can decide between the matter of life, death, and trauma (Woetzel et al., 2018, p.38). In order to reach an adequate response, AI technologies such as smartwatches or voice recognition systems enable users to get help when needed. Some of these technologies even enable the user to submit videos, photos, and text, so the medic gets "an early and clear picture of what to expect" (Woetzel et al., 2018, p.42). When reflecting this current information on the hypothesis introduced at the beginning of the thesis, the second hypothesis comes into mind: *"Monitoring health concerns via current technology increases the probability for quick responses and effective treatment."* For the reason that the technologies such as smartwatches e.g., the apple watch, can track the heart rate as well as the movements including falling, new possibilities of faster diagnosing abnormalities arise (Eadicicco, 2019). With this early detection, the device is able to send the information to the next doctor or emergency medic, which decreases the response time (ibid). Therefore, the second hypothesis can be proven correct. Monitoring patients with e.g., heart conditions by using smartwatches increases the probability of quick responses. As this implementation of the technologies seems to still lie further in the future — at least in Europe — several companies in America and China already try to implement such systems within the daily life, to understand, analyse, predict and prevent certain illnesses.

An example of this effective treatment method and quick response time is the American company "Beyond Verbal" (VocalisHealth, n.d.). The company was established in 2012 and defended their task over the past eight years, becoming an "innovative data company which analysis human voice in real-time and continuously provides insights to the personal health" (Introducing Beyond Verbal—Using voice to save lives, 2017). Thus being said, the data collected from human voice had to be distracted from some AI connected to the IoT. Therefore, the company launched its own developed health monitoring app — the "Beyond Verbal App" (ibid). Within this application, the company programmed algorithms that are able to look for "vocal biomarkers which indicate certain health conditions" of every user, creating a health profile (ibid). This interaction of monitoring and collecting real-time data takes place passively while the analysis for any health conditions are actively evaluated (ibid). Meaning, if something is identified as a health condition/issue, the health care provider, doctor, and the individual itself get an immediate alert (ibid). Through this immediate interaction and detection of any health condition, doctors and the subject have the advantage of a quick and effective treatment (ibid). Therefore, the second part of the 2. hypothesis focusing on effective treatment can assumed to be correct. In this case, the statement can be made that through AI such as monitoring applications — which collect and analyse real-time data — the response time of medics to certain illnesses or emergencies are enhanced as well as the effectiveness of treatment can be improved.

According to Adam Wright — Analyst at "Marktforschungunternehmen IDC" — AI gives humanity also the potential to achieve a better work-life balance and improve free time experiences within daily life. (Eadicicco, 2019). Additionally, he states that the main effect of AI in today's society will rely on services and devices which enable the consumers to stay "fit and healthy" (ibid). Therefore, the focus of AI with a focus on health should not only go after quicker response times and effective treatment but also in the direction of preventing health issues. Therefore, health institutions and AI should focus on the implementation of such AI objects that help to analyse individuals' data, recognising patterns, and make predictions in regards to future health e.g., stress levels.

As these limitations through illnesses do not only arise on a physical level but also in the sector of mental health, the following subchapter will analyse the role of AI in mental health to establish certain possibilities and opportunities to adapt today's treatment styles — improving quality of life.

5.1 The Role of AI in Mental Health

As mental illnesses were introduced in chapter 2.5, it became clear that the diseased individuals (anxiety, depression, or burn-out) showed the characteristic of shying away from "actively seeking help due to what they are experiencing psychological" (Powers, n.d.). Another factor that comes to mind when thinking about the treatment of such illnesses is the lack of therapists, the expensive costs within the healthcare system, and long waiting lists (Kaltenthaler et al., 2008, p.181). With these factors taken into account, untreated mental illnesses can result in negative consequences such as suicide attempts (Powers, n.d.). Therefore, help/support is crucial in order to improve the mental state as well as the quality of life. Finding a "new way to combat depression" as well as the other two illnesses has a great significance to society nowadays and the world at large (ibid). For these particular reasons, several studies and universities, such as the National Institute of Mental Health (NIMH) or MIT, focus on the topic to detect these illnesses. Researchers at MIT developed an especially considerable approach. In order to increase the reliability within this thesis, it was decided to put a specific focus on this conducted case study/experiment from MIT.

The impetus to conduct this case-study was the fact that medical professionals can diagnose depression "by interpreting the responses of individuals to a variety of questions, lifestyle changes, and ongoing thoughts (Hanai et al., 2018, p.1716). Focusing on this therapy method, the researchers from MIT were sure that AI was able to — when correctly programmed — automated the detection of depression (ibid). They found a way "to use neural networks" within AI, which should be used in the experiment to "recognise speech patterns in people that are indicative in depression"(Powers, n.d.). In order to test their newly implemented technology within AI devices, the MIT researches set-up a group of 142 individuals who tested this device (Hanai et al., 2018, p.1716). Different from other technologies, the MIT researchers managed to train the AI, and the algorithms within it too detected depression "through sequential modeling of interaction with mining information on the structure of interviews" (ibid). Through this approach, the model managed to recognise such sicknesses based on a normal conversation "through text or audio rather to response to a pre-set questionnaire" (Powers, n.d). With this found groundwork, the university researchers stood out and made their approach unique (ibid).

32

Within this experiment, the AI model used chains of words or speaking sequences and "analysis whether these speech patterns are more likely to be found in people who are depressed or not" (ibid). Thus being said, the model can be defined as a tool that is not generalised and therefore is able to be implemented in daily devices such as smartphones or voice assistants (ibid). For the reason that this model is able to detect depression symptoms within humans behaviour and speaking patterns, the approach can also be used for the detection of other mental issues such as anxiety and burn-out — especially since these show similar symptoms to depression (Chapter 3.4). This implementation of the model for detecting mental illnesses, especially depression, would allow the AI devices to interfere in humanities' daily life while monitoring peoples' natural conversation, detect potential abnormalities and help in regards to the diagnosis (ibid). Therefore, the difficulty for depressed individuals or subjects with anxiety or burn-out to reach out to help actively and to attain professional attention can be overcome (Hanai et al., 2018, p.1716).

Recalling chapter 1.3, two hypotheses that were made were already supported by previous research. Focusing on the third hypothesis: *"For the reason, AI, IoT, and smart technology increase the possibility of profiling subject health condition status with greater accuracy and predictive outcomes"* — currently the statement can be made that AI in combination with IoT and smart devices establishes the prospect of profiling subject health condition statuses better and more accurately when focusing on mental health conditions. In order to estimate and assess whether such technologies can predict/diagnose such mental issues, more considerations have to be taken into account, such as what data is needed to make such predictions. Therefore, the primary focus within predictive approaches will be concentrating yet again on the already developed software of "Beyond Verbal."

As mentioned before, the application of the company uses the biomarkers within the human voice to identify specific diseases (Introducing Beyond Verbal—Using voice to save lives, 2017). The company goes even a step further and manages through the use of AI in combination with ML and DL processes to make predictive outcomes supporting the approach of the third hypothesis (ibid). 1.2 million patients in the U.S. already use this application "BeyondClinic" — which gives the company itself again the advantage of "extensive databases", enabling their AI to learn from previous data and outcomes, adapting and learning new characteristics in regards to illnesses (ibid). Additionally, the company works "closely with renowned hospitals, insurance, and research institutions globally to create a larger dataset of voice record and correlated medical records" (ibid). Since this approach of Beyond Verbal is focusing on voice recognition systems, it can be stated again that voice assistant and recognition systems are the essential tools in today's "Era of AI." When focusing on health care and voice assistants 1 in 13 consumers using such devices say, "that they have used voice assistants for Health Care," which is likely to rise for the reason of a high demand and low offers on the market (Kinsella & Mutchler, 2019, p. 3). Not only this indicates the rise of voice recognition systems within health care, but also the fact that 50% of voice assistant users — which comprises of around 235 million individuals — would like to use healthcare assistants in the future (ibid). Within this market (HC), implementing applications and solutions should focus on the most used devices: smartphones and smart speakers (Kinsella & Mutchler, 2019, p.9). Since microphones are included everywhere, it gives health companies, doctors, and subjects the opportunity to make use of these and monitor biomarkers in the human voice (ibid). This range of monitoring opportunities gives the health sector a "ready user base that is seven times larger than those that have already employed voice for health care services to date."

Focusing again on diagnosing mental illnesses in the U.S. it becomes clear through the statement of the NAMI (National Alliance of Mental Illnesses) — the average delay between the first mental illness symptoms and treatment usually stands at 11 years (Mental Health By the Numbers | NAMI: National Alliance on Mental Illness, n.d.). One factor that drives up the years for diagnoses and treatment of mental illnesses is the fact that 60% of U.S. counties do not have a single practicing psychiatrist, which makes it nearly impossible for individuals who suffer from these sicknesses to find treatment (ibid). Another factor that makes it difficult for the diseased to receive help is the characteristic of these illnesses, which lets the subjects to be unmotivated and tending to shy away — not reaching out for support (Powers, n.d.). With the implementations such as Beyond Verbal or other voice recognition systems — who are able to analyse emotions and diagnose subjects with mental illnesses, such as anxiety, burn-out, and depression — these obstacles can be overcome. With the opportunity of AI and ML to determine the key behavioural biomarkers within the voice by constantly monitoring the individuals' interaction, the process of diagnosing can be improved (Abbas, 2019). If one individual shies away and is not motivated to go to the doctor, this monitoring and pattern recognition allows the health sector to determine specific characteristics and make suggestions to the subject when certain markers are analysed and recognised. Therefore, the patient does not have to leave the house and reach out for help by themselves anymore. However, the AI gives them the advantage of being diagnosed over different layers of AI learning and contacting an expert, e.g., house visits, or technological interaction via such devices, phone or video.

For this reason, hypotheses two and three come into mind. By using AI and these machine learning processes in the health sector, in this case, mental health, this area can be transformed to the better (Woetzel et al., 2018, p.50). For the reason that these smart devices/AIs such as voice recognition take vital readings in real-time, the collected and analysed data can be transmitted directly to doctors within another location, who can offer further help, e.g., therapy (Woetzel et al., 2018, p.52). This approach, and all the indications mentioned above, such as emotional reading and interpretations, and the ability of AI to contact doctors if necessary, support the statement from the two hypotheses. Therefore, AI is able to diagnose mental illnesses through specific indications within the voice, face, or other physical characteristics. Also, the opportunity to introduce virtual treatment, doctors' appointments, and treatments arise, which creates an entirely new way to approach diseased individuals. Accordingly, a so-called "telemedicine" interactive world will form, where the virtual patient and the virtual physician interact through the audio, visual, or audio-visual device (Woetzel et al., 2018, p. 115). Reflecting hypothesis 1, which was partly supported in Chapter 3.4, the second part — stating, *"New technologies [...] now has the potential to create solutions"* — can be bolstered by the implementations of AI mentioned in previous chapters such as the application of "BeyondVerbal."

As it was specified before, certain obstacles arise when such new technologies are implemented in today's society, especially within the area of cyber risks. However, this is not the only sector companies and cities have to aim their attention at, but also the transformation society has to go through in order for AI in the health sector being successful. Therefore, the next chapter will address this issue taking the "Wave Approach" - by Toffler from Chapter 3.1 into account.

6.0 Societal & Cultural Transformation

As mentioned in the earlier Chapter 3.1: with every significant new invention within our society, a specific new wave starts to build up, swamp over society, and sweep it with it. Therefore, society has to start learning to swim within this new wave and try not to drown. However, before this societal and cultural transformation within the human way of living and mind can take place/can be changed and analysed — the digital transformation has to be introduced. In general digital transformation can be described as every digital technology that is implemented in "areas of a business" as well as daily life (Verdino, 2015). This transformation especially has an impact on the culture and society in regards to further changes (ibid). For example, the implementation of the IoT and the rise of AI, are a step towards another digital transformation — or as Toffler states a constant movement within society (1980).

As mentioned before, in chapter 3.1, it is believed that society currently is yet at another edge of change, and two generations are colliding — Boomers & Gen X vs. Millennials & Gen Z. The "Era of AI" allowed Millennials and Gen Z to grow up with such technology. At the same time, subjects from the Boomer and Gen X Generation had to get used to technology, smart devices, AI, etc. during their lifetime. Children who are raised in a "smart, responsive environment, which is complex and stimulating, may develop different skills" than generations before (Toffler, 1980, p. 191). This difference in skillset also creates the normality/abnormality living in harmony with technology creating issues of broader implementation. According to Toffler, "every civilisation has a hidden code — a setup of rules or principles that run through all its activities like a repeated design" (1980, p.62). To disrupt or change this design and image, gaining trust and have the possibility of widely implementing such technologies (AI) — certain measures have to be taken into account, such as the societal and cultural transformation of humans as well as the shift within the humans' mindset.

When focusing on the human brain — especially the limbic system — it gives the human an unconscious urge to stick to things that they know in order to maintain safety (Berlin, 2018). This urge/unconsciously perceived threat hinders the majority of older generations nowadays from being fully committed to new inventions such as AI. Therefore, it can be stated that humanity itself — at least the older generation — has to transform their minds, including the way "they think about problems and the way they synthesise information" (Toffler, 1980, p.188). According to Toffler, a new transformation/new wave can only take place if the mindset of such generations can be transformed (1980, p.18). Otherwise, either the new invention drowns, or the generation itself is getting stuck in their structure and world view. Therefore, the old assumptions from the previous wave/generation have to be challenged. Focusing on the older generations, most of them — according to Toffler — "do not think about the future and are sure that the world they know will last indefinitely" (Toffler, 1980, p.27). He states that the older generation within a clash of waves mostly finds it difficult to imagine to change/adapt to a different way of life (ibid). As mentioned before, the older generation recognises the things and areas life are changing but "assume that the change will pass by them and that nothing will shake their familiar economic framework" (ibid). This attitude of ignoring changes hinders the transformation/movement into the next wave — "The Era of AI."

In order to overcome/change these beliefs the invention, new technologies and opportunities of implementing such in the daily life have to be communicated transparently to all citizen within smart cities, all patients within the health sector, etc.. To achieve this acceptance organisations should not focus on changing the mindset but to let it grow. The "Growth Mindset" does not only turns its back on a static/single-minded point of view but also enables individuals to develop intelligence (Martinez, 2015). Therefore, leading the older generations away from fear towards a positive image of technology by e.g., showing the benefits through examples, etc. challenges individuals face can be embraced, which leads to the desire to learn more about the subject — reaching for more positive experiences (ibid). For this reason, it can be stated that the central issue of the change/growth in mindset is mainly an issue of age (Cagle, n.d.). Especially when it comes to tolerance in regards to handing over private data. As mentioned in chapter 2.1, the mistrust towards companies from older generations are 10% higher than in the age group of millennials. This issue makes it difficult to engage older generations within movements that include innovations, bringing unfamiliarity. Communicating the use of private data transparently and integrating some boundaries over law enforcement could limit companies accessing only specific data. Therefore, using data primarily for the individuals greater good and not for marketing and manipulation reasons — creates the solution of overcoming the obstacle of mistrust in older generations.

The "Era of AI" is not just a technological revolution but becomes a whole new civilisation/generation (Toffler, 1980, p. 366). This civilisation can be referred to the residents of today and future smart cities, where mostly Millennials, as well as Gen Z, will be active participants in shaping new innovations, cities, and technologies that operate within their daily life and can be used as additional resources (Woetzel et al., 2018, p. 26). This new civilisation with all individual — old as well as younger generations made a start into "The Era of AI" not only the technology itself.

As many experts are focusing on today's implementation and sectors in which AI can find a high acceptance and improve the quality of life, the following chapter will aim its center of attention on such experts and their impressions and experiences with AI in the health sector as well as private usage.

7.0 Expert Interview Analysis

By concentrating on expert interviews in the area of AI, it was decided to contact three different experts to gain diverse insights into various fields. The first expert interview was conducted with Mr. Michael Dehm — an employee of Aon Insurance Company within the Health Insurance market with insights from around the world — followed by Ms. Nicoletta Blaschke — another employee at Aon Insurance Company from the Health Sector with focus on Europe. For the reason that both experts were located in Frankfurt, Germany, the interviews were conducted as a telephone interview. The third and last interview was held in person at the IT University in Hamburg at the Institution of AI. The interview partner was an expert — Dr. Lothar Hotz — who started researching in the field of AI in the early 80s. For the reason that all these interviews took place in Germany, the interview was conducted in German.

Setting up the expert interviews, it was decided to use the same guiding questions for all professionals in order to have the same foundation to build the interview on (Appendix A & B). Additionally, new and different questions arose during the interviews giving a more in-depth insight into certain aspects. Especially interesting about these interviews were the different ideas, personal opinions, and experiences. With the focus on the health sector, diagnosing mental illnesses and obstacles that have to be overcome — diverse perceptions were communicated.

On the one hand, Ms. Blaschke represents the opinion that AI, in general, can be accepted — also from her personally — if certain data privacy law enforcements are given by the government (Blaschke, N. (2019, December 20, ll. 68 - 69). Personal Interview). She states that AI will have a positive impact on the society nowadays but has to be controlled by a higher force (Blaschke, N. (2019, December 20, ll. 111 - 112). Personal Interview). Ms. Blaschke is sure that society will change their perception of AI — similar to smartphones, in the beginning, were nobody though the trend would stick/ older generations saw the invention as an invasion of privacy (Blaschke, N. (2019, December 20,) ll. 112 -113. Personal Interview). Similar to that opinion, Mr. Dehm made his statement. While he counts himself to the older generation (older than Millennials and Gen Z) Dehm states that he shops for example on the internet and knows that all the information: what, to what price and quality — will be continuously tracked (Dehm, M. (2019, December 19, ll.147 - 150). Personal Interview). The important part about this statement is that Mr. Dehm does not mind giving away his personal data — having the same approach to AI in the health sector (Dehm, M. (2019, December 19, l.150 -152). Personal Interview). According to Dehm, nevertheless, he perceives that area of data collection as critical (Dehm, M. (2019, December 19, ll. 152 - 153). Personal Interview). Likewise, Ms. Blaschke, Dehm explains that in order to achieve a high acceptance of AI in health sectors companies and other organisations have to give individuals/human beings the feeling of being in a save area (Dehm, M. (2019, December 19, ll.167 - 172). Personal Interview). This includes convincing subjects about the greater good of collecting such information over AI — for example, through government laws that ensure the certainty that such data will not be used against individuals (Dehm, M. (2019, December 19, ll.387 - 390). Personal Interview) (Dehm, M. (2019, December 19, ll.397 -399). Personal Interview). Thus being said, the statement made earlier in the thesis that AI will find higher acceptance within specific sectors, including high transparency, as well as proper data management by companies implementing cybersecurity, is supported by the two experts.

Another important finding within the three interviews were the supporting statements made in regards to the three hypotheses. According to Mr. Hotz, AI opens many opportunities in several sectors through its ability to adapt by the constant usage/ML (Hotz, L. (2020, January 9 ll. 58 - 63). Personal Interview). He states that through this approach, the machine does not only adapt its processes, but it also takes in its learnings, analyses them, and adapts future processes (Hotz, L. (2020, January 9 ll. 58 - 63). Personal Interview). Additionally to that insight of the AI function Hotz states that through the devices intelligence — the characteristic of pattern recognition — new implementations in sectors such as the health sector to find patterns in e.g., pictures, videos or language arise (Hotz, L. (2020, January 9 ll. 92 - 96). Personal Interview). An example for this implementation within the health sector would be accordingly to Lothar Hotz areas of therapy or diagnostics — transforming the AI system to another tool for doctors as well as patients (Hotz, L. (2020, January 9 ll. 108 - 118). Personal Interview). Focusing on this statement, the first, second, and second hypothesis are supported in regards to creating solutions towards mental illnesses referring to introducing new opportunities for diagnosing these mental illnesses as well as establishing new options of treatments — which underlines earlier research approaches within the thesis.

A similar statement was made by Ms. Blaschke, who is sure that the implementation in the health sector will impact it massively e.g., in radiology (Blaschke, N. (2019, December 20, ll. 148 - 149). Personal Interview). Accordingly to Blaschke AI will be able to support medical doctors with diagnoses as well as with the problem of treating and diagnosing patients faster and from different locations (telemedicine) — overcoming the obstacle of lacking experts (Blaschke, N. (2019, December 20, ll. 151 – 155). Personal Interview). Thus being said, the first, and second hypotheses, are supported focusing on the ability of AI to overcome the obstacle of diagnosing patients faster, as well as improving treatment methods on several levels through inventions such as voice recognition systems. Additionally, Dehm supported these statements with his experience suggesting that AI is a tool that will have a significant impact on the health sector — especially in regards to availability of medical experts, emergency response time and possibilities of treatment — e.g., response for 24 hours a day through the experts in different countries which can be contacted over AI (Dehm, M.(2019, December 19, ll.308 - 314). Personal Interview) (Dehm, M.(2019, December 19, ll.320 - 322). Personal Interview). Focusing on diagnosing mental illnesses within the health sector Dehm states that not only emotions should be taken into account, but also other influences such as early interactions/socialisations of an individual, medical records from family members, etc. in order to improve the accuracy of such diagnoses (Dehm, M. (2019, December 19, ll.437 - 451). Personal Interview) (Dehm, M.(2019, December 19, ll.457 - 458). Personal Interview). Not only does the last statement of higher accuracy through monitoring supports the third hypothesis but also the first and second hypothesis getting stronger support through the last experts' statement.

As it can be seen through the analysis of all three interviews, the experts have a similar opinion on improvements within the health sector through AI in regards to the improvement of treatment and diagnoses through monitoring health conditions of patients — creating more and more solutions. Similar was their point of view on the struggle of collecting private data within the health sector and possible issues within it, nevertheless stating solutions to overcome such struggles. For the reason that AI systems are an extremely new invention when it comes to technologies, future companies/health organisations who want to implement AI in the mental health sector — as well as future researchers — have to take several aspects into account that have not been explored/researched so far.

8.0 Futuristic Outlook

Focusing on future researchers — who will conduct further investigations on the topic of AI, its implementation, and impact within the health sector of mental health — have to take several new aspects into account in order to lay out a path for the technology to gain a foothold in the market.

As one major factor will be the rise of smart cities and the acceptance of society towards facial recognition and voice assistants, researchers should rely on the two technologies when conducting experiments and reaching for a higher level of trust within society. Another possible impact researchers, as well as health organisations, should put an eye on are AI systems that can manipulate/alter emotions within the subconsciousness of the human brain (limbic system & sensor branding). Bringing the advantage of AI being able to analyse and understand emotions within individuals better than humanity itself or subject families — the opportunity to make use of this information arises. For the reason that all these emotions mostly appear on a subconscious level (which makes humanity not aware of them), AI systems could use this information to alter the emotions from e.g., sadness & depression to happiness and joy. With the power of AI detecting emotions, sensing, and monitoring them through smart devices -- health organisation could have the chance of changing the consumers' behaviour/emotions to their improvement of life. For example, by combining emotions to create third emotions such as mentioned in Chapter 2.4 — Neuroscience. Even though such implementation lies in the future, and probably several obstacles arise in regards to the fear of manipulation and monitoring these approaches will appear sooner or later — which is why researchers and health governments should look out for them and start researching in this direction that will profoundly impact our way of living even further.

For the reason that the futuristic outlook, as well as the earlier conducted research extended or supported the thesis approach, hypothesis and statements on an empirical as well as scientific level — the following chapter will discuss all findings and come to a conclusion of the thesis statement and overall findings.

9.0 Discussion and Conclusion

By focusing on the arising problem of mental health issues especially burn-out, anxiety and depression, the downside of lacking experts in certain regions as well as the characteristics of such diseases as being unmotivated to seek help — the research question *"How can AI monitoring aid in the improvement of the quality of life in today's society?"* was developed. The analysis of all chapters and methodologies confirms that approach — that with the implementation of AI, the possibility to improve the individuals' quality of life in the health sector, especially mental health and its opportunities to enhance the prospect of efficient diagnoses, treatment, and fast response can be accomplished. The data suggests that "society itself is influenced by the revolution" of AI and, therefore, their quality of life as well (Chanchaichujit et al., 2019, p.2).

In line with the hypothesis, several correlations and supporting findings were analysed within the thesis. Not only did a study from MIT discover a solution of using AI to detect depression within the human voice through biomarkers but also the company "BeyondVerbal" already makes use of such technologies to diagnose illnesses in an early state and connect a potential patient with a medical expert/doctor (Section 5.1). With the expert interviews taken into account, the hypotheses were supported on another — this time empirical level — strengthening the overall statement of the thesis: "Through the influence of AI, smart technology and IoT the quality of life can be improved."

42

Additionally, the statement of the WHO which describes the purpose of health technology — such as diagnosing mental illnesses through smart speakers — as a tool that is able to solve health problems such as overrun doctors' offices as well as an improvement in quality of life — increases the credibility of the thesis statement and hypothesis (Chanchaichujit et al., 2019, p.131). The research showed that especially the technologies of ML and pattern recognition give AI the possibility to improve diagnoses and treatment within the health sector and mental health. According to the Harvard Business Review, humanity knows more than individuals can tell and cannot even explain exactly "how we're able to do a lot of things" like automating tasks or reading and understanding emotions (Chanchaichujit et al., 2019, p.4). Except for that, humanity nowadays has the opportunity to use AI systems that can achieve such understanding through the technology of ML e.g., diagnosing diseases (ibid). As reported by Annette Zimmerman — the vice president of research at Gartner — "by 2022, your personal device will know more about your emotional state than your own family" (ibid). Precisely this approach was found in the research conducted within the thesis — supporting hypotheses two and three in regards to quick response rate towards an early diagnosis as well as the possibility to profile the patients' health condition more accurately.

Even though several sources and methodologies support these hypotheses, the thesis statement and answers the papers research question — it has to be taken into account that AI is a relatively new technology within our society and has not been implemented in a wider range. Especially within the health sector, which creates a lack of experiments, case studies, and therefore an unknown area for AI experts still have to investigate on many levels. Consequently, it can be stated that the reliability of the paper reflects all relevant findings (till 2020) in regards to the improvement of life within the health sector but can be elaborated in the future when the first steps in the health sector are being realised. Therefore, AI experts should start focusing on conducting more experiments in the field of health. Even more research is needed to establish measures and ways to implement specific data in AI and the ML processes to enable them: creating accurate assumptions in regards to diagnoses as well as focusing on finding acceptance in this sector collecting patients' private data. That is for the reason that if AI systems do not find this acceptance in the health sector and society — such research of AI will be for nothing, and the quality of life of diseased individuals will not be improved.

By keeping the supportive and already conducted research/methodologies, as well as the unknown in mind, the final conclusion can be made that the quality of life of today's society can be improved through AI, such as voice assistants, when implemented in a broader spectrum. That is for the reason that they can diagnose individuals' mental illness e.g., depression — by freeing diseased individuals from being proactive and reaching out for help, minimising response time of e.g., ambulance & treatment and improving the accuracy of diagnoses.

10.0 References

Abbas, N. M. (2019, September 5). *Machine Learning and Mental Health*. Medium. https://towardsdatascience.com/machine-learning-and-mental-health-7981a6001bd5

Akrouf, S., Belayadi, Y., Mostefai, M., & Chahir, Y. (2011). A Multi-Modal Recognition System Using Face and Speech. *International Journal of Computer Science Issues, 8*(3).

Aher, B. (2018, April 20). *How Big Data Impacts Smart Cities—DZone Big Data*. Dzone.Com. https://dzone.com/articles/how-big-data-has-the-biggest-impact-in-smart-citie

Annear, S. (2012, July 24). Dunkin' Donuts Sprays the Smell of Coffee Onto Buses to Increase Sales [Video]. *AmericanInno*. https://www.americaninno.com/boston/dunkin-donuts-sprays-the-smell-of-coffee-onto-buses-to-increase-sales-video/

Artificial Intelligence: The Insights You Need from Harvard Business Review. (2019). Harvard Business Review Press.

Berlin, J. (2018, November 13). Hacking The Human Side Of Digital Transformation. Retrieved January 01, 2020, from https://www.forbes.com/sites/forbescoachescouncil/2018/11/13/hacking-the-human-side-of-digital-transformation/#4688956e394f

Boston Consulting Group. *(2016, October 28). Bridging the Trust Gap: Data Misuse and Stewardship by the Numbers [Business]*. https://www.slideshare.net/TheBostonConsultingGroup/bridging-the-trust-gap-data-misuse-and-stewardship-by-the-numbers

Brodkin, J. (2018, October 11). *Amazon patents Alexa tech to tell if you're sick, depressed and sell you meds*. Ars Technica. https://arstechnica.com/gadgets/2018/10/amazon-patents-alexa-tech-to-tell-if-youre-sick-depressed-and-sell-you-meds/

Brugnara, M., Consonni, C., Foroni, D., Preti, G., Sottovia, P., & Velegrakis, Y. (n.d.). *DATA MANAGEMENT AND SMART CITIES.* 14.

Cagle, K. (n.d.). *AI Augmentation: The Real Future of Artificial Intelligence.* Forbes. Retrieved November 3, 2019, from https://www.forbes.com/sites/cognitiveworld/2019/09/30/ai-augmentation-the-real-future-of-artificial-intelligence/#2f9105a2393e

Case Studies. (n.d.). *Research-Methodology.* Retrieved January 20, 2020, from https://research-methodology.net/research-methods/qualitative-research/case-studies/

Chanchaichujit, J., Tan, A., Meng, F., & Eaimkhong, S. (2019). *Healthcare 4.0—Next Generation Processes with the latest technology.* Palgrave McMillan.

Chapter 2: Research Methodology . (n.d.). Retrieved 2020, from https://shodhganga.inflibnet.ac.in/bitstream/10603/3704/12/12_chapter 2.pdf

Cmar, R. (n.d.). *The three biggest challenges to building a commutable smart city.* Smart Cities World. Retrieved October 10, 2019, from https://www.smartcitiesworld.net/opinions/opinions/the-three-biggest-challenges-to-building-a-commutable-smart-city

Combination of Emotions. (2018). [Letter to Sina Kiene].

Cole, A. H. (2014). "Anxiety," in *Encyclopedia of Psychology and Religion*, ed. D. A. Leeming. (Boston, MA: Springer), 95–99. doi: 10.1007/978-1-4614-6086-2_38

Cooper, D. C. (n.d.). Introduction to Neurosciences (Vol. 1).

Cronshaw, R. (2014, January 15). *An Introduction to Neuroscience.* Oxford Summer School from Oxford Royale Academy. https://www.oxford-royale.com/articles/introduction-neuroscience.html

Eadicicco, T. W. and L. (2019, May 8). *KI macht unseren Alltag schon heute viel einfacher – aber die große Revolution kommt erst noch.* Business Insider Deutschland. https://www.businessinsider.de/wie-ki-programmierung-unseren-alltag-heute-deutlich-erleichtert-2019-8

Freudenberger, H. J. (1974). Staff burn-out. *J. Soc. Issues* 30, 159–165. doi: 10.1111/j.1540-4560.1974.tb00706.x

Hamill, H. (n.d.). *Interview Methodology—Sociology—Oxford Bibliographies—Obo.* Retrieved January 20, 2020, from https://www.oxfordbibliographies.com/view/document/obo-9780199756384/obo-9780199756384-0105.xml

Hanai, T.A., Ghassemi, M.M., & Glass, J.R. (2018). Detecting Depression with Audio/Text Sequence Modeling of Interviews. *INTERSPEECH.*

Harrison, H., Birks, M., Franklin, R., & Mills, J. (2017). Case Study Research: Foundations and Methodological Orientations. *Forum Qualitative Sozialforschung / Forum: Qualitative Social Research, 18*(1). https://doi.org/10.17169/fqs-18.1.2655

Introducing Beyond Verbal—Using voice to save lives. (2017, August 5). https://www.youtube.com/watch?v=1nL0w79zBY0

Kinsella, B. (2018a, January 8). *56 Million Smart Speaker Sales in 2018 Says Canalys.* Voicebot.Ai. https://voicebot.ai/2018/01/07/56-million-smart-speaker-sales-2018-says-canalys/

Kinsella, B. (2018b, October 10). *Amazon Files for Patent to Detect User Illness and Emotional State by Analyzing Voice Data—Voicebot.ai.* https://voicebot.ai/2018/10/10/amazon-files-for-patent-to-detect-illness-by-analyzing-voice-data/

Kinsella, B. (2019a, September 24). *Smart Speaker Sales to Rise 35% Globally in 2019 to 92 Million Units, 15 Million in China, Growth Slows.* Voicebot.Ai. https://voicebot.ai/2019/09/24/smart-speaker-sales-to-rise-35-globally-in-2019-to-92-million-units-15-million-in-china-growth-slows/

Kinsella, B. (2019b, October 17). *Amazon Continues to Lead in Smart Displays with 59% Share While Facebook Portal Only Tallies 2% Adoption Among Smart Speaker Users.* Voicebot.Ai. https://voicebot.ai/2019/10/17/amazon-continues-to-lead-in-smart-displays-with-59-share-while-facebook-portal-only-tallies-2-adoption-among-smart-speaker-users/

Kinsella, B. (2019c, October 29). *More Than Half of Consumers Want to Use Voice Assistants for Healthcare—New Report from Voicebot and Orbita.* Voicebot.Ai. https://voicebot.ai/2019/10/29/more-than-half-of-consumers-want-to-use-voice-assistants-for-healthcare-new-report-from-voicebot-and-orbita/

Kinsella, B., & Mutchler, A. (2019). *VOICE ASSISTANT CONSUMER ADOPTION IN HEALTHCARE* (p. 37) [PDF]. VOICEBOT.AI.
Koutsimani, G., Montgomery, A., & Georganta, K. (2019). The Relationship Between Burnout, Depression, and Anxiety: A Systematic Review and Meta-Analysis. *Frontiers in Psychology*, *10*, 19. https://doi.org/10.3389/fpsyg.2019.00284

Kolb, B., & Wishaw, I. Q. (2016). *An Introduction to Brain and Behavior* (5th ed.). New York, NY: Worth.

Koutsimani, G., Montgomery, A., & Georganta, K. (2019). The Relationship Between Burnout, Depression, and Anxiety: A Systematic Review and Meta-Analysis. *Frontiers in Psychology*, *10*, 19. https://doi.org/10.3389/fpsyg.2019.00284

Kuehn, K. (2013, February 12). *The limbic system, the cognitive mind and the user illusion that misleads.* SmartCompany. https://www.smartcompany.com.au/marketing/the-limbic-system-the-cognitive-mind-and-the-user-illusion-that-misleads/

Kumar, S. U., & Prakash, A. (2016). *International Journal of Science and Research. 5*(2), 11. https://doi.org/10.21275/v5i2.nov161007

Lim, C., Kim, K.-J., & Maglio, P. P. (2018). Smart cities with big data: Reference models, challenges, and considerations. *Cities, 82,* 86–99. https://doi.org/10.1016/j.cities.2018.04.011

Lindstrom, M. (2008). Buy-ology: how everything we believe about why we buy is wrong. New York , New York: Crown Business.

Literature Reviews—The Writing Center. (n.d.). Retrieved January 20, 2020, from https://writingcenter.unc.edu/tips-and-tools/literature-reviews/

Martinez, E. (2015, May 2). *5 powerful ways to transform mindset.* People Matters. https://www.peoplematters.in/article/talent-assessment/5-powerful-ways-transform-mindset-11145?utm_source=peoplematters&utm_medium=interstitial&utm_campaign=learning s-of-the-day

McFadden, C. (2019, March 17). *Can Technology Cause Anxiety and Depression?* https://interestingengineering.com/can-technology-cause-anxiety-and-depression

Mental Health By the Numbers | NAMI: National Alliance on Mental Illness. (n.d.). Retrieved January 12, 2020, from https://www.nami.org/learn-more/mental-health-by-the-numbers

Mental Health Facts in America. (n.d.). Retrieved January 21, 2020, from https://www.nami.org/nami/media/nami-media/infographics/generalmhfacts.pdf

Neurocomputing. (2017). *253,* 104–114. https://doi.org/10.1016/j.neucom.2017.01.096

Pathak, N., & Bhandari, A. (2018). *IoT, AI and Blockchain for .NET:Building a Next-Generation Application from the Ground Up.* Apress.

Pedrycz, W., & Shyi-Ming, C. (Eds.). (2018). *Computational Intelligence for pattern recognition* (1st ed.). Springer International Publishing.

Polzin, T. S., & Waibel, A. H. (n.d.). *Detecting Emotions in Speech. 7.*

Powers, A. (n.d.). *AI Can Identify Depression Based On A Natural Conversation, An MIT Study Finds.* Forbes. Retrieved November 3, 2019, from https://www.forbes.com/sites/annapowers/2018/09/30/ai-senses-depression-in-people-based-on-how-they-talk-an-mit-study-finds/

Santoro, T. (2019, October 9). Emperical Social Research—Fundamentals I: Emperical research, research process, quantitive vs. Qualititive research, quality criteria [PDF]. Methodology, Hamburg, Germany.

Snyder, H. (2019). Journal of Business Review. *Elsevier, 104,* 333–339. https://doi.org/DOI: 10.1016/j.jbusres.2019.07.039

Spielberger, C. D. (1966). *Anxiety and Behavior.* Academic Press.

Tansu, O. (2018). *Brand Psychology.* Brand Psychology, Hamburg, Germany.

Taulli, T. (n.d.). *AI (Artificial Intelligence) Words You Need To Know.* Forbes. Retrieved November 3, 2019, from https://www.forbes.com/sites/tomtaulli/2019/09/07/ai-artificial-intelligence-words-you-need-to-know/#11deec60406a

Toffler, A. (1980). *The Third Wave* (1st ed.). Morrow.

Twenge, J. M., Cooper, A. B., Joiner, T., E. Duffy, M. E., & Binau, S. G. (2017). Journal of Abnormal Psychology. *Https://Www.Apa.Org,* 185–199.

Valenzuela, D., & Shrivastava, P. (n.d.). *Interview as a Method for Qualitative Research.* 20.

Verdino, G. (2015, March). What is Digital Transformation, Really? Retrieved January 20, 2020, from https://www.gregverdino.com/digital-transformation-definition/

Vocalis Health. (n.d.). Vocalishealth. Retrieved November 13, 2019, from http://www.beyondverbal.com/

Wegrzyn, M., Vogt, M., Kireclioglu, B., Schneider, J., & Kissler, J. (2017). Mapping the emotional face. How individual face parts contribute to successful emotion recognition. Plos One, 12(5), 1–15. doi: 10.1371/journal.pone.0177239

What is Neuroscience? (n.d.). Retrieved December 13, 2019, from https://www.allpsychologycareers.com/topics/neuroscience.html

Wegrzyn, M., Vogt, M., Kireclioglu, B., Schneider, J., & Kissler, J. (2017). Mapping the emotional face. How individual face parts contribute to successful emotion recognition. *PLoS ONE, 12*. https://doi.org/10.1371/journal.pone.0177239

Woetzel, J., Remes, J., Boland, B., Lv, K., Sinha, S., Strube, G., Means, J., Law, J., Cadena, A., & von der Tann, V. (2018). *SMART CITIES: DIGITAL SOLUTIONS FOR A MORE LIVABLE FUTURE* (pp. 1 - 152) [PDF]. McKinsey. https://www.mckinsey.com/~/media/mckinsey/industries/capital%20projects%20and%20infrastructure/our%20insights/smart%20cities%20digital%20solutions%20for%20a%20more%20livable%20future/mgi-smart-cities-full-report.ashx

11.0 Appendix

11.1 Appendix A: Interview questions in German

German

1) Wie ist Ihre allgemeine Haltung zur KI im alltäglichen Leben?
2) Haben Sie schon einmal bewusst Berührungspunkte mit einer KI gehabt?
   1) Wie war Ihre Erfahrung?
3) Es wird momentan ja viel in die Richtung der Möglichkeiten der KIs' geforscht und ich würde jetzt einfach mal behaupten, dass dies die nächste große Erfindung für die Menschheit ist, nach der letzten großen Erfindung des Handys. Wie stehen Sie zu dieser Aussage?
4) KI bietet immer mehr Möglichkeiten im alltäglichen Leben. Welche Bereiche, denken Sie, werden am meisten von der Implementierung der KI betroffen sein?
5) In welchem Bereich sehen Sie die KI als Innovation?
6) Wie denken Sie, dass die KI im Gesundheitswesen eingegliedert werden kann?
7) Welche Bereich wird das im Gesundheitssektor Ihrer Meinung betreffen?
8) Was sind Ihrer Meinung nach die Schattenseiten der KI, wenn diese im Gesundheitswesen implementiert werden?
9) Was sind die Hürden der KI, wenn diese im deutschen Gesundheitswesen eingesetzt werden? Oder gibt es überhaupt welche?
10) Es gibt ja schon einige KIs', wie Gesichtserkennung und Spracherkennung, die die Emotionen eines Menschen lesen können. Wie schätzen Sie den Einsatz von solch einer Technologie in Depressionsprävention und Erkennung ein?
11) Mentale Krankheiten, wie Depressionen, Burn-out und Anxiety werden ja oft durch ein weniger ausgeglichenes Leben ausgelöst/getriggered. Besonders in der heutigen Zeit, wo ein Individuum 24 h 7 Tage die Woche zu erreichen ist. Wie denken Sie, kann die KI dort eingesetzt werden, um entgegen der Krankheit zu wirken?
12) Wenn man auf die Forschung von KIs' blickt, ist zu erkennen, dass in den letzten Jahrzehnten in diesem Sektor sehr viel geschehen ist. Unter anderem gibt es in Amerika auch schon Firmen, wie z.B. Beyond Verbal, die durch smart devices über die Stimme das Gesundheitsbild der Kunden tracken und Krankheiten dadurch präventiv hervorsagen können. Auch Forschungen haben schon belegt, dass KIs' sich zukünftig nicht auf die

Heilung, sondern auf die Prävention von Krankheiten konzentrieren werden. Wie stehen Sie zu dieser Aussage?

13) Wenn man auf vorherige technische Innovationen blickt, lässt sich erkennen, dass sich die Gesellschaft dahingehend angepasst/transformiert hat. Was muss Ihrer Meinung nach in der Gesellschaft heutzutage passieren, so dass diese Angehensweise der KI im Gesundheitssektor durch Tracking im privaten Alltag breitflächig eingesetzt werden kann?

14) Wie kann diese Technologie Akzeptanz in der Gesellschaft finden?

11.2 Appendix B: Interview Questions in English

English

1) What is your general perception of AI in the daily life?
2) Have you ever consciously used an AI?
    1) Please describe your experience?
3) Currently, a significant amount of research is focused on the potentialities of AI. I would even say that this is the next big paradigm shift for humanity after the last great invention of the mobile phone. What do you think about this statement?
4) AI is offering more and more possibilities to be used in the daily life. Which areas do you think will be most affected by the implementation of AI?
5) In which areas do you see AI as an enhancement?
6) How do you think AI can be implemented in the health sector?
7) In which specific areas of the health sector?
8) In your opinion what are the downsides of AI when implemented in the health sector?
9) What would be the obstacles of AI when integrated in the German health sector? Or are there none?
10) There are already some AIs such as face and voice recognition that can read and interpret an individual's emotions. How do you rate the use of such technology in depression prevention and detection?
11) Mental illnesses such as depression, burn-out and anxiety are often triggered by a less balanced life style. Especially in today society where an individual can be reached 24 hours 7 days a week. What do you think AI could do in order to counteract in the direction of the disease?
12) If one considers the research of AIs, one recognises that in the last decades a significant amount has occurred. Among other things, there are already companies in America, such as "Beyond Verbal", which uses smart voice technology to track customers' health and prevent illness. Research has also shown that AI will not focus on healing but disease prevention in the future. What do you think about this statement?
13) When looking at previous technological innovations, it can be seen that society has adapted / transformed itself in adapting to this invention. What do you think must happen in society today, so that this approach of the AI tracking data in private lives (within the health sector) can be widely used?

14) How can this technology find acceptance in current society?

11.3 Appendix C: Interview 1 with Michael Dehm

1   00:00:00

2   **Sina Kiene:** Hallo, Herr Dehm, hier spricht Sina Kiene.

3

4   00:00:05

5   **Michael Dehm:** Es hat geklappt, ich habe ja gerade Ihre Mail gesehen.

6

7   00:00:05

8   **Sina Kiene:** Ja, ich sitze hier auch gerade im Büro und habe Sie auch versucht mit der

9   Durchwahl zu erreichen. Das hat irgendwie nicht geklappt.

10

11   00:00:17

12   **Michael Dehm:** Ja, es ist ganz komisch. Dass mit der Durchwahl versuche ich auch

13   grundsätzlich nie, weil das immer irgendwie nicht funktioniert. Man muss leider immer

14   mühsam die Nummer einwählen.

15

16   00:00:28

17   **Sina Kiene:** Ja, wahrscheinlich wird es daran gescheitert sein. Na ja, auf jeden Fall erst

18   mal vielen Dank, dass Sie sich die Zeit heute für mich nehmen und an meinem

19   Bachelorthema interessiert sind. Soll ich noch einmal kurz erklären, worum es überhaupt

20   geht und was meine Bachelorarbeit umfasst?

21

22   00:00:41

23   **Michael Dehm:** Genau. Wenn Sie mich da ganz kurz mal einstimmen. Ich bin schnell

24   nochmal über die Fragen vorhin geflogen und dann konnte ich mich wieder daran

25   erinnern, dass ich schon mal gelesen habe, dass Sie künstliche Intelligenz als generelles

26   Thema gewählt haben. Aber wenn Sie mir noch ein bisschen Hintergrund geben, das wäre

27   schön.

28

29   00:00:54

30   **Sina Kiene:** Ja, genau. Also ich fokussiere mich sozusagen bei meinem Bachelor auf die

31   Frage "Wie kann künstliche Intelligenz durch das Monitoring die Qualität des Lebens

32   verbessern?". Und meiner Meinung nach kann es das durch die künstliche Intelligenz,

33   durch die Smart-Technologie und durch das Internet of Things sehr vorantreiben. Durch
34   Daten-Kollektion, dadurch dass man jetzt auch Alexa benutzt und man das Handy ständig
35   bei sich hat. Ich persönlich denke, wir haben verschiedene Persönlichkeiten, also einmal
36   unsere reale Persönlichkeit: Wir wissen wer wir sind, wie wir im täglichen Leben sind,
37   dann einmal unsere soziale Identität sozusagen einmal auf Social Media, wie wir möchten
38   dass Leute uns sehen und dann einmal sozusagen die Geister-Identität, das heißt die Daten
39   die wir nicht genau wissen, die wir weggeben. Wenn wir mit der Kreditkarte bezahlen
40   oder wenn wir Google-Maps benutzen. Darauf fokussiert sich zum größten Teil meine
41   Bachelor-Arbeit.

42

43   00:02:02
44   **Michael Dehm:** Habe ich verstanden.

45

46   00:02:04
47   **Sina Kiene:** Ich kann ja auch einmal zu meinen Hypothesen einiges sagen. Ich glaube
48   zum Beispiel, dass man durch künstliche Intelligenzen Krankheiten, wie Depressionen
49   oder ähnliches gezielt diagnostizieren kann, indem man Emotionen beeinflussen und
50   lesen kann.

51

52   00:02:24
53   **Michael Dehm:** Gibt's ja medizinisch auch schon Evidenz?

54

55   00:02:28
56   **Sina Kiene:** Es gibt ein paar Firmen in den USA. Eine heißt Beyond Verbal, die haben
57   eine App entwickelt, die die ganze Zeit die Kommunikation des Trägers der App
58   sozusagen trackt. Und die können aus der Stimme lesen, ob derjenige
59   Stimmungsschwankungen hat und tatsächlich auch schon einige Herzinfarkte
60   hervorsehen. Darauf habe ich mich noch nicht konzentriert, weil ich mich eher auf die
61   mentale Ebene fokussieren möchte.

62

63   00:02:58
64   **Michael Dehm:** Ja, aber ich würde das grundsätzlich auch für möglich halten, dass es
65   Möglichkeiten der Wahrnehmung und der Auswertung gibt, die sagen wir mal, ein
66   Normalsterblicher nicht ohne weiteres vornehmen kann, aber was mit Unterstützung von

67 Technologien und auch anderen Sensoren, darum geht es ja auch am Ende, dass man da
68 irgendwie Dynamik in der Stimme herausfiltern kann, die dann mit anderen Mustern
69 verglichen werden, die solche Dinge auswerten können. Ich habe jetzt kürzlich mal einen
70 Bericht gesehen, da war ein Hund in der Lage über seine Witterung herauszufinden, ob
71 jemand an Parkinson erkrankt ist. Und zwar nicht nur schon klar und offensichtlich
72 erkrankt ist an Parkinson, sondern er hat das zwei Jahre vorher schon wittern können und
73 das war das eigentlich Interessante daran. Sie spielen ja auch hier sehr stark auf
74 Prophylaxe, dass bei einer sehr frühen Erkennung bei vielen Krankheiten man noch ganz
75 erfolgreich gegensteuern kann und die haben das mit Hund ausgetestet und er hat das
76 immer wieder bestätigen können. Und dann hat er es bei einer Person nicht bestätigen
77 können und die ist zwei Jahre später an Parkinson erkrankt. Das war der witzige Zufall
78 auch in dieser Versuchsanordnung, dass der Hund eine Wahrnehmung hatte. Man geht
79 davon aus, dass es irgendwas mit Geruch zu tun hatte. Er hatte eine Wahrnehmung, die
80 man mit hiesiger Technologie noch gar nicht erreichen konnte, was aber nicht heißt, dass
81 man mit Technologie und da sind wir dann auch wieder bei künstlicher Intelligenz (wenn
82 man das weiter verfeinert) nicht irgendwann in der Situation ist, dass vielleicht auch
83 künstliche Intelligenz über Duftstoffe herausfinden können, ob jemand in zwei, drei
84 Jahren Parkinson oder Alzheimer oder sonst irgendetwas bekommt.
85
86 00:05:13
87 **Sina Kiene:** Ja, genau.
88
89 00:05:14
90 **Michael Dehm:** Insofern bin ich fest davon überzeugt, dass wir auch in den nächsten
91 Jahren noch mit Dingen konfrontiert werden, die wir uns jetzt im Moment noch gar nicht
92 vorstellen können, weil es hier überwiegend immer nur um Data Analytics und um
93 wiederkehrende Vorgänge geht. Aber ich glaube je besser auch Sensorik wird, also
94 optische Erkennung, Geruchserkennung oder Stimmen lesen zu können, desto besser wird
95 auch das Zusammenspiel mit der künstlichen Intelligenz und es wird noch einmal ganz
96 andere Anwendungsformen geben.
97
98 00:05:55
99 **Sina Kiene:** Ja, das glaube ich nämlich auch. Zum Beispiel in Südkorea hatte Dunkin-
100 Donuts auch einmal eine Kampagne. Bei dieser wurde in Bussen Kaffeegeruch versprüht.

101 Immer wenn die Dunkin-Donuts-Werbung im Radio lief, hat die KI das festgestellt und
102 den Kaffeegeruch dann versprüht. Durch die Kombination aus Geruch und
103 Radiowerbung konnte Dunkin-Donuts den Umsatz um 18 Prozent steigern.

104

105 00:06:17

106 **Michael Dehm:** Da sind wir auch gleich schon bei der anderen Seite, auf die wir sicher
107 auch zu sprechen kommen. Manipulationsmöglichkeiten. Ok, aber ich habe verstanden.
108 Finde ich ein sehr spannendes Thema. Deswegen habe ich auch gerne gesagt, da mach
109 ich mal mit.

110

111 00:06:37

112 **Sina Kiene:** Das freut mich sehr. Das ist für mich auch nicht so einfach Experten zu
113 finden, muss ich sagen. Auch als wir unser Gespräch am Telefon hatten: Sie haben sehr
114 interessante Ansichten und ich finde, das macht einen Experte aus.

115

116 00:06:52

117 **Michael Dehm:** Es könnte auch einfach meine Reflektionen darstellen. Ich nehme auch
118 gerne das Expertenkompliment an.

119

120 00:07:00

121 **Sina Kiene:** Sehr gut. Genau, sonst können wir einfach gleich in die Fragen einsteigen.
122 Es entwickelt sich aber auch automatisch ein Gesprächsfluss. Starten wir mit der ersten
123 Frage: Wie ist Ihre allgemeine Haltung zur KI im alltäglichen Leben?

124

125 00:07:17

126 **Michael Dehm:** Ich bin ja Jahrgang 64 und bin kein Digital Native. Insofern muss ich
127 sagen, dass ich im Verhältnis zu meinen Kindern (einen Sohn mit 15, eine Tochter mit
128 20) im Grunde keinerlei Berührung habe. Also ich benutze auch keine Alexa und ich
129 würde das auch nicht benutzen. Das macht mir keinen Spaß, muss ich ganz ehrlich sagen.
130 Also nicht, dass ich gegen KI als solche wirklich Vorbehalte hätte. Ich kenne ganz viele
131 interessante Anwendungsbereiche. Das finde ich auch ganz toll, wenn sich die Dinge
132 etablieren. Aber ich bin in meinem Leben irgendwie so routiniert unterwegs, mit der Art
133 und Weise wie ich Dinge bisher immer gemacht habe und mir sind persönliche Kontakte
134 auch viel wichtiger, als alles Digitale. Insofern würde ich mein Digitalisierungsgrad nicht

135   wirklich gezielt erweitern wollen. Was nicht heißt, dass ich da irgendwas ganz interessant
136   finde und für mich nützlich finde, dass ich das unter Umständen auch machen würde, aber
137   ich gehöre nicht zu den Leuten, die per se nur, weil es jetzt irgendeine digitale Version
138   von irgendetwas gibt oder eine KI-Version da sofort drauf anspringen würde. So ist meine
139   Haltung aber offen. Für mich sehe ich da keinen Automatismus und bis ich mich von
140   meinen Routinen, meinen analogen Routinen entferne, das dauert bei mir immer.
141

142   00:09:05

143   **Sina Kiene:** Also Sie haben keine Hemmungen, dass da die Daten weggegeben werden
144   oder man Sie manipulieren könnte?

145

146   00:09:10

147   **Michael Dehm:** Nein, da ich ja auch im Internet unterwegs bin und dort auch Sachen
148   kaufe, ist mir völlig bewusst, dass ich damit meine Konsumgewohnheiten, wann ich was
149   von welchem Hersteller und in welcher Qualität und zu welchem Preis kaufe, dass ich da
150   natürlich komplett getrackt bin. Das macht mir jetzt nichts aus, also auch die Themen, die
151   dann kommen: Gesundheitsdaten und so weiter und so fort. Ich bin ein überaus
152   gesundheitsbewusster Mensch. Ich hätte damit auch gar keine Probleme. Ich würde es
153   trotzdem grundsätzlich nicht unkritisch sehen, weil man sich ja auch ausrechnen kann,
154   was am Ende damit passiert. Und wenn ich mal das negative Ende der Skala aufzeige,
155   dass es möglicherweise Menschen geben könnte, die, man müsste es mal zweistufig
156   formulieren, die keine Krankenversicherung mehr bekommen würden, wenn sie nicht
157   bereit sind sich tracken zu lassen - mit all ihren Gewohnheiten und wenn sie sich dann
158   tracken lassen, dass man dann feststellt, das ist ja so ein negativer Kandidat, der kriegt
159   entweder trotzdem keine Versicherung oder er müsste so unfassbar viel für diese
160   bezahlen. Das würde etwas sein, was ich mit Sorge sehen würde. Wir haben ja viele
161   Bereiche in unserem täglichen Leben, die von einem Kollektivgedanken geprägt sind und
162   auch letzten Endes getragen werden. Künstliche Intelligenz führt natürlich zu einer
163   unglaublichen Möglichkeit selektiv zu sein und das könnte für die, die sich in einem
164   positiven Raster wiederfinden, ganz toll werden. Aber es könnte für andere Teile der
165   Bevölkerung, die da aus welchen Gründen auch immer nicht in einem Raster sind, bitter
166   werden. Eine generelle Aussage zu diesem Thema bzw. Frage kommt ja auch noch einmal
167   zu einem späteren Zeitpunkt ihres Fragenkataloges. Also wäre ich extrem positiv für das
168   ganze Thema und ich sehe alle großen Vorteile, die man damit haben könnte. Aber das

169 Akzeptanzthema in der Gesellschaft aus Frage 14 (Appendix B), wird in hohem Maße
170 damit korrespondieren, dass man den Menschen das Gefühl gibt, die KI kann nicht gegen
171 sie verwendet werden. Zum Beispiel könnte es gesetzliche Regeln geben, die
172 sicherstellen, dass es nicht gegen sie verwendet werden kann.

173

174 00:11:50

175 **Sina Kiene:** Okay und was glauben Sie, wäre es der einzige Weg KI so zu etablieren,
176 dass die große Gesellschaft sagen würde: Wir implementieren KI in unser alltägliches
177 Leben, ohne dass wir Sorgen haben?

178

179 00:12:03

180 **Michael Dehm:** Das weiß ich nicht. Wir haben ja bei Aon so eine Well-One App, kennen
181 Sie die schon?

182

183 00:12:09

184 **Sina Kiene:** Nein, davon habe ich noch gar nicht gehört.

185

186 00:12:11

187 **Michael Dehm:** Im Bereich Health Solutions. Über diese Well-One App, da können Sie
188 Mental Wellbeing, Financial Wellbeing, Health Wellbeing; alles Mögliche können Sie
189 dort tracken. Das korrespondiert auch mit diesen variables von Fitbit. Also da kann man
190 sehen, wie viele Schritte man gegangen ist, wie lang man geschlafen hat, wie lang die
191 Tiefschlafphase war, wie lang die REM-Phase war, also all das. Das habe ich mal meinen
192 Kindern gezeigt. Die fanden das natürlich sofort großartig, weil sie sagten: "Ah ja und
193 dann sehe ich, dass ich nicht genug gelaufen bin und dann kann ich noch eingeben, was
194 ich am Tag gegessen habe, dann bekomme ich einen optimierten Diätplan, dann
195 bekomme ich irgendwie Hinweise, dass ich dies machen sollte und das machen sollte und
196 so". Ich denke, dass ist wahrscheinlich Generationsspezifisch. Sie sind ja auch ein junger
197 Mensch und sind damit großgeworden. Sie haben viel schneller eine Begeisterung dafür.
198 Ich glaube, je jünger die Leute werden, desto höher ist die Akzeptanz oder die
199 Bereitschaft sich darauf einzulassen. Je geringer ist die Sorge, dass es auch
200 missbräuchlich verwendet werden könnte, aber es kommt natürlich auch am Ende des
201 Tages dazu, dass man immer sagt, die Daten sind anonym und dann erfährt keiner etwas.
202 Na gut, so naiv kann man dann sein, aber es gibt natürlich auch Mittel und Wege dann an

203 Daten doch heranzukommen und dann kann es Ihnen auch passieren, dass Sie irgendwo
204 entweder nicht befördert werden oder dass Sie keinen Arbeitsplatz mehr bekommen, weil
205 Sie nachweislich einfach schon so viel Fehltage beim letzten Arbeitgeber in den letzten
206 drei Jahren hatten und ich glaube, ich sage es noch einmal: Ich finde die Technologie
207 faszinierend, ich finde, dass was man damit machen kann, ist ausgesprochen nützlich,
208 aber es gibt halt unglaublich viele Missbrauch Szenarien. Aber es ist in den Händen von
209 Unternehmen und Industrie, die in allererster Linie ein kommerzielles Interesse und kein
210 altruistisches Interesse haben, was dazu führen kann, dass man in seinen
211 Kaufgewohnheiten manipuliert wird, dass man keine Verträge bekommt, keinen
212 Mietvertrag, keinen Krankenversicherungsvertrag, keine Autoversicherung. Also ich
213 habe ein Auto, das trackt alles. Ich habe so einen großen Volvo, der ist komplett
214 durchdigitalisiert. Der misst jedes Mal, wenn ich auf der Autobahn über dem Speed Limit
215 fahre, er misst, wenn ich zu nah auffahre. Da denke ich mir: Naja gut halb so wild, das
216 sehe ja nur ich. Wenn ich mir jetzt überlege diese Daten, weil das Auto ist ja auch
217 irgendwie permanent vernetzt, diese Daten würden an meinen Kfz-Versicherer
218 übermittelt: Dann würde der mir im nächsten Jahr den Vertrag nicht verlängern, so wie
219 ich manchmal Auto fahre. Und trotzdem wissen Sie, ich fahre seit 35 Jahren unfallfrei,
220 das stünde ja dagegen, dass ich sage: Ich war zwar nicht immer regelkonform, aber ich
221 kann halt relativ gut fahren. Es gibt ja so eine Bandbreite zwischen Schwarz und Weiß,
222 was KI produziert, weil das es nun mal ein primäres Instrument unserer
223 Lebenswirklichkeit ist und da glaube ich, sind Menschen meiner Generation tendenziell
224 eher misstrauisch und jüngere Menschen sind da eher sorgloser.
225
226 00:15:48
227 **Sina Kiene:** Ja. Ja, das sehe ich auch so, dass einfach die Generationen da
228 aufeinandertreffen. Die Gesellschaft ist einfach in einem großen Umschwung.
229
230 00:15:56
231 **Michael Dehm:** Ich sage Ihnen noch etwas. Vielleicht für Sie auch ganz interessant. Ich
232 war mal vor ein paar Jahren auf einer Aon Konferenz in Florida. Da war abends als
233 Keynote Speaker ein sogenannter Futurist, also Zukunftsforscher. Und er sagte in der
234 Zukunftsforschung unterscheidet man grundsätzlich zwei Bereiche: Nämlich einmal die
235 Dinge, wo wir sagen müssen - das könnte kommen, wir wissen es aber noch nicht genau
236 und es gibt die Bereiche, wo man sagt - wir wissen ganz genau, dass es kommt, aber es

237   nur eine Frage der Zeit ist. Und KI und diese ganzen Anwendungsbereiche, von denen

238   ich eben gesprochen habe, das ist für mich relativ sicher, dass das alles kommen wird und

239   es ist nur eine Frage der Zeit. Es wird in dem einen oder anderen Land, wie in den USA

240   zum Beispiel früher kommen. Es wird in Ländern, die sehr hohe Datenschutzschwellen

241   haben, wie in Kontinentaleuropa, Deutschland, Frankreich, schwerer durchsetzbar

242   werden. Aber es wird dann doch irgendwann kommen, weil ich glaube, dass einfach der

243   Wettbewerb / Wettbewerbsdruck, sehr hoch sein wird, dass man auch als Unternehmen

244   ohne KI in Zukunft gar nicht mehr existieren kann.

245

246   00:17:08

247   **Sina Kiene:** Das ist wirklich sehr interessant, dass es Techniken gibt, wo man vielleicht

248   noch nicht sicher ist, ob die kommen und bei einigen es nur eine Frage der Zeit ist.

249

250   00:17:19

251   **Michael Dehm:** Ganz genau. Und KI gehört für mich definitiv zu den Themen, die eine

252   große Erfolgsstory hervorbringen werden. Ja, es gibt ein ganz interessantes Unternehmen

253   in Kanada. Das heißt Trade Desk. Da habe ich mal vor 1 Jahr ein paar Aktien gekauft,

254   weil ich das sehr interessant fand. Das Unternehmen arbeitet mit den Großen - Amazons

255   und Facebook zusammen. Wenn sie heute auf Amazon gehen und haben jetzt nach einem

256   Rasenmäher geguckt und haben dabei keinen gekauft, dann eine Woche später suchen Sie

257   nach einem Pullover und auf einmal erhalten Sie bei Amazon auf der rechten Seite immer

258   wieder Rasenmäher-ADs. Sehr wahrscheinlich auch schon erlebt. Also diese ganze

259   Logik, die dahintersteckt, ist ja nichts anderes als künstliche Intelligenz und das macht

260   Trade Desk. In Zeiten wo Werbung, nicht wie in meiner Generation in erster Linie über

261   eine Zeitung oder über das Fernsehen kam, sondern wo das Internet eigentlich die

262   Hauptplattform ist, um gezielt Werbung an Menschen heranzubringen, wird natürlich

263   künstliche Intelligenz unfassbar wichtig. Unternehmen, die sich darauf spezialisieren

264   werden enorm erfolgreich werden. Ich kann Ihnen das gerade mal zeigen oder ich sage

265   Ihnen das mal, können Sie sich mal angucken. Unter Trade Desk in Kanada und New

266   York gehandelt. Jetzt sage ich Ihnen mal, wie die Firma sich in einem Jahr entwickelt hat.

267   Da können Sie auch mal nachlesen, was die Firma macht. Es ist künstliche Intelligenz,

268   nix anderes. Vor einem Jahr stand der Aktienkurs der Firma bei 102 Dollar pro Aktie. Ein

269   Jahr später, also heute stehen diese auf 289, fast verdreifacht. Daran können Sie schon

270   sehen, auch die Investoren glauben an künstliche Intelligenz.

271   00:19:55

272   **Sina Kiene:** Das entwickelt sich wirklich in alle Richtungen. Und wenn man jetzt auf den
273   Gesundheitssektor schauen würde, wo glauben Sie, dass die KI am meisten eingesetzt
274   wird. Also eher im Krankenhaus oder im privaten Leben?
275

276   00:20:15

277   **Michael Dehm:** Ich könnte mir das sehr gut vorstellen, weil ich glaube, wir leben ja auch
278   in so einer Gesellschaft, wo Dinge immer perfekter werden müssen, wo man gerne auch
279   Statistiken hat. Das ist ja auch die jüngere Generation, zu der Sie gehören. Wenn ich das
280   bei meiner Tochter sehe, da müssen immer perfekte Bilder auf Facebook sein und so
281   weiter und so fort, das hat eine enorme Relevanz und wenn man dann noch sagen kann,
282   diese Woche bin ich 10.523 Schritte gelaufen, also schon 100 Prozent mehr, als in der
283   letzten Woche, ich glaube dafür gibt es eine Faszination und das wird die privaten Daten
284   erfassen, Statistiken zu machen, sich auch untereinander messen zu können. Es geht ja
285   nicht nur darum, sich selbst zu disziplinieren, sondern auch in einer virtuellen
286   Wettbewerbssituation mit anderen zu sein. Sie müssen ja nicht mal gegen jemanden
287   rennen, Sie müssen ja eigentlich nur noch ihre Daten hinterher vergleichen und jeder
288   könnte auf der anderen Seite des Globus laufen. In dem privaten Anwendungsbereich und
289   auch was Sie vorhin da gesagt haben, mit Alexa, was die dann möglicherweise an
290   Einsatzmöglichkeit noch alles mit sich bringt. Das wird eine starke Entwicklung sein. Ich
291   glaube, dass es im Gesundheitsbereich wahrscheinlich noch viel ausgeprägter sein wird.
292   Also gerade für Versicherungen, wo ja das Gesetz der großen Zahl und wo Statistik eine
293   hohe Relevanz hat, wird das ganz, ganz starke Einsatzbereiche haben. Insofern, da sind
294   Sie mit Ihrer Bachelorarbeit und die Richtung in die Sie da forschen, wirklich gut
295   unterwegs. Ich denke, das ist ein ganz spannender Trend.
296

297   00:22:09

298   **Sina Kiene:** Vielen Dank.

299

300   00:22:11

301   **Michael Dehm:** Es gibt ja auch ganz viele Unternehmen, die sich damit beschäftigen,
302   überwiegend Amerikaner muss man sagen. Sie haben ja hier Beyond Verbal schon
303   genannt, die auf die u.a. auf die Digitalisierung von Gesundheitsleistungen abzielt und
304   insgesamt ein großes Thema darstellt. Ich kann Ihnen noch zwei Unternehmen nennen,

305 die ich auch eher als Investor beobachte. Das eine heißt Intuitive Surgical und das andere
306 heißt Teladoc. Intuitive Sugical, das ist ein Unternehmen, was mikroinvasive Chirurgie
307 betreibt, wo man dann mit einem ganz kleinen Dinge in ihr Knie reingeht und dann
308 irgendwas macht. Das Gerät wird mit einem Joystick bedient. Aber jetzt können Sie sich
309 eigentlich vorstellen, vielleicht gibt es gar nicht so viele Ärzte oder viele, die das können.
310 Vielleicht gibt es gar nicht so viele Ärzte überall auf der Welt. In Zukunft muss man
311 vielleicht nach Afrika, in irgendein hygienisch einwandfreies Krankenhaus, wo man nur
312 eine Maschine hinstellt und der Arzt kann aus New York aus seinem Wohnzimmer die
313 OP machen. Allein was das an Möglichkeiten eröffnet, zum Beispiel braucht man viel
314 weniger Leute, die viel weniger reisen müssen.
315
316 00:23:42
317 **Sina Kiene:** Naja, man ist auch einfach global flexibler.
318
319 00:23:45
320 **Michael Dehm:** Total, total. Man könnte ja sagen, solche Ärzte werden in Zukunft nur
321 noch in einem Land ausgebildet, in einem Haus, die 24 Stunden rund um die Uhr rund
322 um die Welt operieren können. Das ist theoretisch schon möglich. Mit so einem Gerät
323 können Sie natürlich nicht alle OPs mitmachen, aber auch das ist nur eine Frage der Zeit,
324 da wird es immer mehr Anwendungsmöglichkeiten geben. Und die Firma Teladoc ist im
325 Grunde der Arzt über den Bildschirm.
326
327 00:24:16
328 **Sina Kiene:** Zum Beispiel habe ich dann eine Sitzung mit einem Arzt in Amerika und
329 nicht in der Arztpraxis.
330
331 00:24:25
332 **Michael Dehm:** Was ja auch durchaus Sinn macht. Sie können, wenn Sie eine schwere
333 Verletzung hatten, die Erstversorgung vor Ort haben und in der Woche danach kann man
334 gucken, ob die Wunde sich gut geschlossen hat. Da reicht es, wenn der Arzt sich das auf
335 dem Bildschirm anguckt indem Sie Ihr Handy darauf halten. Dann müssen Sie nicht 100
336 Meilen dafür fahren. Ist ja totaler Unsinn. Ich bin ja im Bereich Health Solutions tätig.
337 Mittlerweile kann ich sagen, dass der größte Kostentreiber für Unternehmen die
338 Krankenversicherung von Mitarbeitern auf der ganzen Welt ist. In Deutschland ist es ja

339	anders, weil da zahlt ja jeder seine Krankenversicherung selbst, also der Arbeitgeber zahlt
340	ja nur einen Anteil. Aber in vielen Ländern auf der Welt können sich Normalsterbliche
341	überhaupt keine Krankenversicherung leisten, wenn ihr Arbeitgeber das für sie nicht
342	bezahlt. Das ist in den USA sehr ausgeprägt, das ist auch in Ländern wie Brasilien oder
343	Singapur ganz extrem. Die Medizinkosten, die steigen in solchen Ländern im Schnitt
344	jedes Jahr um zehn Prozent. Und wir reden ja über Millionen von Prämien für das ein
345	Unternehmen bezahlt. Wenn Sie da sehen, wie die Kosten davon galoppieren, dann sind
346	das natürlich auch alles Themen, die schon deswegen wichtig sind, weil man damit
347	natürlich auch Kostenkontrolle hat und Kosten stabil halten kann.
348	
349	00:28:05
350	**Sina Kiene:** Na ja, wie gesagt, ich sehe auch einen ganz großen Faktor im
351	Gesundheitswesen. Glauben Sie denn, dass die Firmen später dann KIs auch benutzen
352	werden, um zu gucken, ob die Work-Life-Balance von unseren Mitarbeitern gut ist oder
353	wie können wir diese verbessern. Zum Beispiel durch Sportangebote in der Mittagspause.
354	
355	00:28:34
356	**Michael Dehm:** Ich bin sogar sicher, dass es so kommen wird und zwar aus dem
357	einfachen Grund, weil die Unternehmen das Problem haben werden, dass sie immer
358	weniger gut qualifizierte Leute finden. Das wird dazu führen, dass man um die,
359	Stichworte War for Talent, immer mehr werben muss und potentiellen Mitarbeitern
360	immer bessere Arbeitsbedingungen verschaffen muss. Insofern glaube ich schon, dass die
361	Unternehmen solche Dinge/Informationen sammeln werden, auswerten werden und
362	zusehen werden, dass sie für Mitarbeiter, die sie unbedingt halten wollen, versuchen
363	werden, ein besseres Wellnessangebot anzubieten. Das hat natürlich auch irgendwo seine
364	Grenzen. Wen man mit den HR-Leuten spricht, finden diese ein Wellnessangebot
365	natürlich toll. Der CFO wird aber behaupten, dass dafür kein Geld da ist. Das ist natürlich
366	immer eine Frage, wie groß ist da der Druck und welche Möglichkeiten hat ein
367	Unternehmen. Aber vom Grundsatz her glaube ich sehr wohl, dass das ein intensives
368	Thema werden wird. Ich hatte ja auch, als ich Mitglied des People Teams war, alle 2 Jahre
369	einen kostenlosen Gesundheitscheck, der ging den ganzen Tag. Das gehört ja auch dazu.
370	
371	
372	

373   00:30:08

374   **Sina Kiene:** Also glauben Sie, dass es eher auf Prävention später abzielt, was wir schon

375   angesprochen hatten?

376

377   00:30:16

378   **Michael Dehm:** Also Prävention und Selektion. Prävention im Idealfall, natürlich ja.

379   Wenn Sie die Informationen haben, können Sie natürlich auch überlegen, ob Sie in

380   irgendjemanden noch investieren wollen, wenn der auf einmal mit seinen Daten nicht

381   mehr so gut dasteht.

382

383   00:30:34

384   **Sina Kiene:** Ja, das stimmt. Das sind dann immer die zwei Seiten der Medaille.

385

386   00:30:37

387   **Michael Dehm:** Naja und da sind wir wieder bei dem Punkt, den ich vorhin angesprochen

388   habe mit der Sicherheit, die man den Menschen geben muss. Es müsste auf irgendeine

389   Art und Weise sichergestellt sein und zwar gesetzlich, dass die Daten nicht

390   missbräuchlich verwendet werden können. Ich mache Ihnen mal ein Beispiel: Ich bin ja

391   Jurist von der Ausbildung her. Sie können ja in einem Strafverfahren zum Beispiel

392   manchmal Beweise nicht gegen jemanden verwenden, wenn sie auf unzulässige Art und

393   Weise gesammelt worden sind. Das ist in den USA noch viel ausgeprägter. Sie können

394   im Grunde nur in der Situation sein, dass Sie sagen, mit dem Beweis könnte ich jemanden

395   überführen, der ein Mörder ist. Aber ich darf den Beweis nicht verwenden und der Richter

396   und die Geschworenen müssen das ignorieren. Das gibt es ja so und wenn man den

397   Gedanken jetzt weiterdenkt, könnte man sagen: Die Informationen, die wir da

398   einsammeln, die dürfen nur zum Wohle der Leute verwendet werden, aber nicht zu ihrem

399   Nachteil.

400

401   00:31:46

402   **Sina Kiene:** Dann sollte die KI also nicht zur Manipulationen im Marketing verwendet

403   werden?

404

405

406

407 00:32:02

408 **Michael Dehm**: Es ist ja auch ein subtiles Thema. Irgendwann wird die KI das
409 Unterbewusstsein der Leute wahrscheinlich auf eine brillante Art und Weise
410 manipulieren. Die KI sagt ja nicht, kauft jetzt Donuts, sondern die Leute haben
411 irgendwann die Assoziation Donuts und Kaffee. Jedes Mal, wenn sie irgendwo einen
412 Kaffee riechen, denken sie jetzt könnte ich eigentlich auch ein Donut dazu essen. Das ist
413 ja das was passiert. Und es gab schon vor vielen, vielen Jahren, als die Menschheit noch
414 nicht so digitalisiert war, Versuche, dass man bei Werbesendungen einen ganz normalen
415 Werbeclip eingespielt hat. Sie wissen ja, dass so eine Sequenz von zehn Sekunden, die
416 besteht ja, sag ich mal aus 1000 Bildern und wenn Sie da in diesen 1000 Bildern zweimal
417 in einem gewissen Abstand ein Eis eingebaut haben, dann haben Sie das eigentlich nicht
418 bewusst gesehen, aber Ihr Unterbewusstsein hat das Eis wahrgenommen. Das hat man an
419 Leuten getestet, die einmal den Film ohne das Eis und einmal den Film mit dem Eis
420 gesehen haben. Die Leute, die den Film mit den Eissequenzen gesehen haben, hatten viel
421 größeren Drang dazu, sich ein Eis zu kaufen. Das ist ja ein sehr altes, sehr analoges
422 Beispiel, wenn Sie so wollen, wie leicht man über Unterbewusstsein Konsumverhalten
423 manipulieren kann. Das ist ja auch ich meine, wir reden jetzt immer nur von
424 Konsumverhalten, man kann vieles andere natürlich damit entsprechend auch
425 manipulieren. Und das ist auch einfach wieder die Down Side. Wie kann man als
426 Gesellschaft sicherstellen, dass die Industrie, die in erster Linie natürlich ein
427 kommerzielles Interesse hat, solche Optionen nicht gegen die Leute verwendet?
428
429 00:34:17

430 **Sina Kiene:** Glauben Sie denn, dass dann die KI später darauf abzielen kann Emotionen
431 unterbewusst zu beeinflussen? Ich meine das passiert ja prinzipiell im Kaufverhalten, wie
432 Sie eben schon berichtet haben.
433
434 00:34:36

435 **Michael Dehm:** Ich denke, dass das möglich ist. Sie haben ja auch hier die Frage zu
436 diesen ganzen emotionalen Themen: Depressionserkennung, Burn-out, Früherkennung
437 und so weiter und so fort. Bei all den Sachen muss man ja sehen, dass es immer ein
438 Zusammenwirken ist aus Dingen gibt, die aus einer frühen Sozialisation kommen und
439 einer Lebenssituation, die aufeinanderprallen. Aus dieser Kombination kann dann eben
440 eine pathologische Situation werden oder eben nicht. Nicht jeder, der aus seiner Kindheit

441 heraus ein Trauma hat, der muss deswegen später depressiv werden oder Burn-out
442 bekommen. Es müssen immer mehrere Dinge zusammenkommen, sodass es aus der
443 Sozialisation kommt. Das können Sie ja schon mal nicht mehr abstellen. Mit ihrer
444 Prophylaxe können sie sozusagen nur sicherstellen, dass jemand jetzt nicht in eine
445 Lebenssituation kommt, die dann eben eine Depression triggert. Wie macht man das oder
446 wenn man es sagen könnte, man kann in dem Frühstadium das vielleicht schon erkennen,
447 also wie wir vorhin gesagt haben Parkinson. Sagen wir mal, wir würden jetzt eine
448 Depression als eine psychische Erkrankung und Parkinson als eine physiologische
449 Erkrankung gleichstellen, weil man auch sagen könnte, vielleicht hat doch eine
450 Depression irgendetwas mit der biochemischen Prädisposition im Körper zu tun. Das
451 weiß man ja alles auch heute noch gar nicht so genau.

452

453 00:36:21

454 **Sina Kiene:** Ja, das ist ja alles noch gar nicht weitgehend genug erforscht.

455

456 00:36:23

457 **Michael Dehm:** Dann könnte man sicherlich sagen, dass man damit auch im Sinne von
458 Prophylaxe und Früherkennung auch etwas erreichen kann. Man könnte ja auch zum
459 Beispiel in einem Interview sagen, das ist vielleicht wofür derjenige sich bewirbt, nicht
460 die passende Aufgabe für ihn. Da hat er vielleicht viel zu viel Stress oder zu viel
461 Verantwortung. Es liegt ihm alles überhaupt gar nicht. Das könnte man vielleicht mit
462 einer in 20 Jahren möglichen Iris Diagnostik erkennen.

463

464 00:36:58

465 **Sina Kiene:** Ja, Pupillenerweiterung

466

467 00:37:00

468 **Michael Dehm:** Ja, ich weiß nicht. Kennen Sie den Film Blade Runner?

469

470 00:37:07

471 **Sina Kiene:** Ja, ich bin ein großer Fan von Action Movies.

472

473 00:37:13

474 **Michael Dehm:** Kennen Sie den alten Blade Runner aus 1984?

475   00:37:15

476   **Sina Kiene:** Ja, kenne ich.

477

478   00:37:19

479   **Michael Dehm:** Gut. Da gibt es ja auch diesen Worldkampftest am Anfang und da gibt

480   es die Irisdiagnostik. Sie sieht, ob einer lügt oder ob es eine emotionale Reaktion gibt.

481   Das Auge lügt nicht. So, also jetzt könnte man natürlich sagen, wenn man das

482   weiterentwickelt, dann kann man Menschen in Zukunft zielgerichteter einsetzen. Das

483   wäre eine tolle Prophylaxe.

484

485   00:37:50

486   **Sina Kiene:** Sozusagen in der Berufswahl.

487

488   00:37:51

489   **Michael Dehm:** Es gibt bei Versicherungsmakler 35 verschiedene Aufgaben. Die KI

490   könnte dann zum Beispiel sagen, der ist partout kein Feldmensch, sondern ist eher ein

491   Fachspezialist. Das könnte ja durchaus sein, dass es dafür emotionale Parameter gibt, die

492   die Eignung für die eine Aufgabe stärker ausprägen, als andere. Es gibt mittlerweile auch

493   Unternehmen, die ihre Interviews auf diese Art und Weise durchführen. Sie beziehen zum

494   Beispiel Facebook etc. mit in den Prozess ein. Da hat man ja auch schon festgestellt, dass

495   diese Auswertungen über künstliche Intelligenz zuverlässiger sind, als ein persönliches

496   Interview.

497

498   00:38:45

499   **Sina Kiene:** Ja, Wahnsinn.

500

501   00:38:47

502   **Michael Dehm:** Die Art und Weise, wie Sie sich auf Facebook präsentieren, lässt

503   unglaublich viel Rückschlüsse auf Sie zu und zwar viel mehr, als Sie denken, auch wenn

504   Sie sich in einem Interview so gut verkaufen, wie sie nur können. Mit der Unterstützung

505   von KI kann man diese Datenmassen effizienter und auf eine objektivere Art und Weise

506   auswerten.

507

508

509   00:39:30

510   **Sina Kiene:** Ja, das stimmt. Dann wird man während des Interviews auch nicht

511   aussortiert, nur weil man etwas Falsches anhat.

512

513   00:39:37

514   **Michael Dehm:** Man könnte sagen, unsere KI guckt nicht, ob derjenige geputzte Schuhe

515   anhat, sondern die KI guckt wirklich nur auf die Gesichtsparameter.

516

517   00:39:46

518   **Sina Kiene:** Ja, mega spannend. Ich bin gespannt, wie sich die KI in den nächsten Jahren

519   so weiterentwickeln wird.

520

521   00:39:56

522   **Michael Dehm:** Ich glaube, das können wir uns überhaupt gar nicht vorstellen. Das wird

523   alles in fünf Jahren so viel weiter sein, als wir uns heute in unserer Fantasie vorstellen

524   können.

525

526   00:40:11

527   **Sina Kiene:** Das bewegt sich ja auch alles viel, viel schneller, wenn man so zurückdenkt

528   an die Industrialisierung. Das hat ja alles so seine Zeit gebraucht. Aber dann auf einmal

529   kamen die Technik und Computer, sodass große Entwicklungsschritte über Jahrzehnte

530   gemacht werden/wurden. Zum Beispiel wurde innerhalb von zehn Jahren das große

531   Handyformat mit wenig Software in ein kleineres Handy mit komplexeren Anwendungen

532   entwickelt. Das sind wirklich große Fortschritte.

533

534   00:40:32

535   **Michael Dehm:** Ja, absolut.

536

537   00:40:36

538   **Sina Kiene:** Sie meine Fragen alle ausführlich und gut beantwortet. Vielen Dank dafür.

539

540

541

542

543   00:40:45

544   **Michael Dehm:** Ich habe noch ein paar Minuten Zeit. Gucken Sie gerne noch einmal

545   über Ihre Unterlagen, ob Ihnen zu irgendeinem Thema noch etwas fehlt. Ich habe jetzt

546   auch nur so munter vor mich her geplaudert und habe auf die Fragen gar nicht mehr

547   geguckt.

548

549   00:40:55

550   **Sina Kiene:** Vielleicht tatsächlich noch eine Frage. Es gibt ja bereits sehr viele KI -

551   Anwendungen. Besonders Gesichtserkennung und Spracherkennung können teilweise ja

552   schon Emotionen lesen. Es ist auf jeden Fall präziser mit beiden zusammen, als nur mit

553   einer Anwendung zu arbeiten. Glauben Sie, dass diese KI weitgehend in Kliniken

554   eingesetzt werden könnten oder auch im privaten Haushalt oder auf Straßen? Hier kann

555   man ja auch die Kriminalitätsbekämpfung mit ins Boot holen.

556

557   00:41:26

558   **Michael Dehm:** Wollte ich gerade sagen. Es gibt ja auch Psychologen, die können aus

559   der Mimik erkennen, ob jemand zu einer bestimmten Frage lügt oder nicht, oder ob eine

560   bestimmte Frage eine bestimmte Emotion, wie Angst oder Wut oder sonst irgendetwas

561   auslöst. Ich glaube, wenn man sich noch mehr im Klaren darüber ist, welche Bewegung

562   im Gesicht jetzt genau welchen Schluss zulässt, dann kann man auch einen Computer

563   oder eine Software programmieren, die das total perfekt erkennt. Das glaube ich schon

564   und das wäre etwas in der konkreten Anwendung. Aber das wäre natürlich auch rein

565   theoretisch möglich, dass Sie in der U-Bahn unten eine Kamera haben und dass diese

566   schon irgendwie erkennen kann: Er hat einen bösen Gesichtsausdruck. Den müssen jetzt

567   mal rausfischen. Thema öffentliche Sicherheit, ist sicherlich etwas was in Zukunft viel,

568   viel stärker auch mit künstlicher Intelligenz arbeiten wird. Das ist dann Rasterfahndung

569   und somit auch eine Form der KI. Diese sammeln Daten weltweit ein, legen diese

570   übereinander und kommen dann zu Erkenntnissen, dass einer genauso gereist ist, wo an

571   fünf verschiedenen Stellen Auftragsmorde erfolgt sind. Auf einmal können KI's

572   erkennen, der müsste es eigentlich gewesen sein. Und dann vernetzen die KI's das mit

573   irgendwelchen Daten, die Sie über jemanden haben und dann schnappen sie denjenigen.

574   Das ist die Kriminalitätsbekämpfung, ein Riesenthema und es findet natürlich seine

575   Grenze beim Datenschutz. Das ist die größte Herausforderung.

576

577 00:43:30

578 **Sina Kiene:** Das heißt, wenn die Regierung einfach ein bisschen den Datenschutz,
579 besonders hier in Deutschland, öffnen würde, wäre es auf jeden Fall für die Firmen
580 einfacher, KI's auf den Markt zu bringen oder anderen Firmen anzubieten.

581

582 00:43:41

583 **Michael Dehm:** Klar, ich meine die Sicherheitsbehörden würden das heute alles schon
584 kaufen, wenn man es verwenden dürfte. Aber es ist nicht so einfach.

585

586 00:43:54

587 **Sina Kiene:** Wahrscheinlich wird die erste Entwicklung wirklich in Amerika stattfinden.
588 Die USA haben ja schon viele Sicherheitssysteme, auch gesundheitlich mit den Apps, die
589 wirklich alles aufzeichnen können.

590

591 00:44:05

592 **Michael Dehm:** Da würde ich Ihnen fast widersprechen wollen, weil, wer allen
593 davonlaufen wird, wird China sein.

594

595 00:44:13

596 **Sina Kiene:** China habe ich jetzt nicht mit auf dem Schirm gehabt.

597

598 00:44:16

599 **Michael Dehm:** Ja, aber das ist natürlich so, weil dort Themen wie Datenschutz und
600 Persönlichkeitsrechte einfach überrollt werden, wenn es dem Großen und Ganzen dient.
601 Und die Art und Weise wie dort Daten gesammelt werden, über Personen und ausgewertet
602 werden, ob sie sich Wohl verhalten und dann dafür auch die Möglichkeit erhalten eine
603 Zweizimmerwohnung oder ein Auto zu kaufen. Es ist ja dort alles schon Realität.

604

605 00:44:45

606 **Sina Kiene:** Ja, ich meine, China hat jetzt sogar ein Punktesystem für jeden Einwohner
607 eingeführt.

608

609

610

611   00:44:49

612   **Michael Dehm:** Genau, das ist genau das, was ich meine. Das werden wir erleben, dass

613   China viel, viel schneller und viel, viel konsequenter in diesen Dingen handelt. Und das

614   wird auch das, was ich vorhin gesagt habe, bewirken, dass der Druck auf den Rest der

615   Welt enorm groß wird. Es wird in bestimmten Teilbereichen natürlich dazu führen, dass

616   China enorme Wettbewerbsvorteile gegenüber anderen Ländern hat. Die werden einfach

617   bestimmte Probleme mit Härte und Konsequenz besser lösen, als der Rest der Welt und

618   dann wird der Rest der Welt irgendwann sagen: Leute jetzt müssen wir mal gucken, ob

619   wir total zurückfallen wollen oder ob wir nicht mit unseren Datenschutzrechten vielleicht

620   doch ein bisschen salopper umgehen müssen. Das ist eher im großen Bild.

621

622   00:45:41

623   **Sina Kiene:** Ich meine auch vor allem Deutschland hängt ja mit Technologien relativ

624   weit hinterher, was z.B. die Verbindung mit dem Internet angeht. Auch die

625   Entscheidungen unserer Regierung spielt eine große Rolle. Zum Beispiel hat sie jetzt erst

626   vor fünf Jahren ein internetbasiertes Department eingeführt. Das ist relativ spät. Da bin

627   ich mal gespannt, ob man als Land noch aufholen kann oder das Schlusslicht bleibt.

628

629   00:46:11

630   **Michael Dehm:** Ja, absolut. Aber es ist eine große Herausforderung. Ich habe mal den

631   ehemaligen amerikanischen US-Botschafter Jeff Kornblum getroffen. Ich hatte mal das

632   Vergnügen, mit ihm und meinem damaligen Chef ein längeres Gespräch zu führen. Bei

633   meinem amerikanischen Chef, als ich noch bei der ERG war und Jeff Kornblum, der

634   schon seit über 30 Jahren in Deutschland lebt und beide Kulturen, die amerikanische und

635   die deutsche und die europäische gleichermaßen gut kennt, hat gesagt:" der größte

636   Unterschied zwischen meinem Heimatland, den Amerikanern und den Europäern oder

637   auch insbesondere Deutschland ist, dass Deutschland ist eine konsensuale Gesellschaft

638   ist. Bei uns sind nur Dinge durchsetzbar, die einen breiten gesellschaftlichen Konsens

639   haben. Eine Regierung würde sich nichts anderes trauen. Aus welchen Gründen auch

640   immer. Entweder, weil sie zutiefst Demokraten sind oder weil sie nur Angst haben, die

641   nächste Wahl nicht mehr zu gewinnen. Das lasse ich jetzt mal dahingestellt. Aber das ist

642   der große Unterschied zu den Ländern wie die USA und auch China, wo Dinge dann im

643   Zweifel einfach gemacht werden.

644

645   00:47:23

646   **Sina Kiene:** Das Risiko wird aber eingegangen.

647

648   00:47:27

649   **Michael Dehm:** Das ist der Trial Error und wenn es dann halt mal schiefgelaufen ist,

650   dann hat es halt ein paar Tausend Leute erwischt, dann korrigiert man es wieder. In

651   Deutschland würde man nicht loslaufen, wenn das Risiko bestünde, ein paar Tausend

652   Leuten zu schaden. Das ist in der Tat auf der einen Seite das, was uns auch auszeichnet

653   als Kultur und als Gesellschaft. Das verschafft uns im Wettbewerb mit anderen vielleicht

654   auch einen großen Nachteil.

655

656   00:47:56

657   **Sina Kiene:** Ich finde das Thema hochinteressant und blicke erwartungsvoll in die

658   Zukunft. Wie Sie schon meinten, in den nächsten fünf Jahren wird es wahrscheinlich

659   unsere Vorstellungen von heute übertreffen.

660

661   00:48:09

662   **Michael Dehm:** Klar, weil sich die Rechnerkapazitäten verdoppeln werden und das alle

663   zwei Jahre.

664

665   00:48:15

666   **Sina Kiene:** Heutzutage hat die KI ja schon wahnsinnige Kapazitäten und interagiert ja

667   nicht nur mit Menschen, sondern auch untereinander.

668

669   00:48:25

670   **Michael Dehm:** Absolut. Die Potenziale aus diesen Vernetzungen, das kann man

671   überhaupt noch gar nicht absehen. Da fehlt mir auch die Vorstellungskraft. Aber als

672   Resümee würde ich immer sagen, die Technologie kommt. Die Frage ist, wie schnell sie

673   bei uns ankommt. Es gibt ja unglaublich viele positive Anwendungsbereiche zur

674   Implementierung. Je mehr man in der Gesellschaft eine Überzeugung dafür entwickeln

675   kann, dass die KI kontrollierbar ist und sie nicht gegen die Menschen verwendet werden

676   kann, desto einfacher wird der Einführungsprozess. Das ist natürlich immer ein Problem.

677   Wenn alle diese Technologien rein deutsch wären, würden die Leute das auch eher

678 glauben. Dadurch, dass es im Grunde in dem Bereich keine Landesgrenzen mehr gibt, ist
679 es natürlich schwieriger.
680
681 00:49:20
682 **Sina Kiene:** Ja, auf jeden Fall.
683
684 00:49:23
685 **Michael Dehm:** Über das Internet kommt ja jeder aus Myanmar oder sonst irgendwoher,
686 in jedes Wohnzimmer. Das sehen Sie ja auch in China. Dort werden ja auch viele Sachen
687 einfach aus dem Internet zensiert und finden ja gar nicht mehr statt.
688
689 00:49:42
690 **Sina Kiene:** Die Einwohner von China haben ja auch gar keinen Zugriff auf die ganzen
691 sozialen Medien, die wir haben. Die Einwohner haben ein eigenes zusammengefasstes
692 Programm. Ich glaube, das heißt WeChat. Da sind alle Medien in chinesischer Form
693 enthalten.
694
695 00:49:56
696 **Michael Dehm:** Ja, ganz genau. Das ist so und ich meine auch solche Unternehmen sind
697 natürlich in diesen Ländern echte Giganten. WeChat, das gehört ja zu einer Gesellschaft
698 Tencent und mittlerweile eines der 20 größten Unternehmen auf der Welt. Sie haben eine
699 Marktkapitalisierung von, ach nee die ist noch klein. Entschuldigung habe ich
700 verwechselt. Immerhin auch zwölf Milliarden.
701
702 00:50:41
703 **Sina Kiene:** Das ist nicht wenig. Ich meine, die haben ja jetzt auch in China Alibaba. Das
704 ist hier ähnlich wie Amazon, die fahren schon große Geschütze in Bezug auf
705 Konkurrenzunternehmen. Sie haben mir sehr viele und interessante Aspekte für mein
706 Bachelorthema gegeben, sodass wir das Interview hier gerne beenden können.
707
708 00:51:07
709 **Michael Dehm:** Ich hoffe, das war hilfreich für Sie. Wieviel Leute interviewen Sie denn
710 insgesamt?
711

712 00:51:11

713 **Sina Kiene:** Insgesamt drei Leute. Ich interviewe noch einen Professor von dem
714 Künstlichen-Intelligenz-Institut hier aus Hamburg und noch eine Kollegin von Ihnen,
715 Nicoletta Blaschke.

716

717 00:51:23

718 **Michael Dehm:** Ah ja, die sitzt hier bei mir in Frankfurt. Es gibt ja hier in Frankfurt das
719 erfolgreichste KI Unternehmen zumindest hier in Deutschland, wenn nicht sogar in ganz
720 Europa. Die Firma heißt Arago. Den CEO, den habe ich mal kennengelernt, vor zwei
721 Jahren, auf einer Veranstaltung, das ist der Chris Boos. Den finden Sie aber, wenn Sie auf
722 die Seite gehen. Er sieht aus wie ein Albino und zwar aus dem Grund, weil er auch einer
723 ist. Der ist fast blind, aber das ist ein Frankfurter Bub und er hat diese Kappé aus dem
724 Boden gestampft. Die haben mittlerweile auch Büros im Silicon Valley, in China, in
725 Singapur. Sina, also unfassbar erfolgreich und die machen nichts anderes als künstliche
726 Intelligenz.

727

728 00:52:18

729 **Sina Kiene:** Ja, Wahnsinn. Vielleicht versuche ich den CEO tatsächlich noch mal zu
730 kontaktieren. Der kann mir vielleicht auch nochmal ganz gute Insights geben.

731

732 00:52:26

733 **Michael Dehm:** Ich habe Boos als Speaker mal auf einer Veranstaltung gesehen. Der
734 erzählte eine tolle Geschichte, natürlich erzählt er extrem positiv und das ist ja vielleicht
735 auch was, was wir jetzt noch gar nicht abgedeckt haben, weil wir hier im
736 Gesundheitssektor unterwegs waren. Aber die große Angst der Menschen vor künstlicher
737 Intelligenz ist ja auch die, dass künstliche Intelligenz unglaublich viele Arbeitsplätze
738 vernichtet. Und dann ist natürlich immer das Argument, dass künstliche Intelligenzen
739 natürlich nur die banalen Arbeitsplätze vernichten und dafür die Leute mehr Zeit haben
740 für kreative Arbeit. Hier muss man natürlich auch mal realistisch sehen, so viele kreative
741 Arbeit gibt es auch nicht und viele Menschen leben eben davon, dass sie mit ihrer
742 niedrigen Qualifikation relativ einfache Tätigkeiten ausführen. Ich kann Ihnen sagen, ich
743 habe Freunde in großen Anwaltskanzleien, da geht man davon aus, dass künstliche
744 Intelligenz wie z.B. die Software KIRA – eine KI für Rechtsanwaltskanzleien in Zukunft
745 die Tätigkeiten in großen Kanzleien um 40 Prozent reduzieren wird.

746   00:53:41

747   **Sina Kiene:** Die Entwicklung ist wirklich verrückt. Aber ich glaube auch, dass neue

748   Technik/Technologien dann auch wieder neue Arbeitsplätze schaffen. Da öffnen sich

749   auch ganz andere Sektoren sozusagen.

750

751   00:53:50

752   **Michael Dehm:** Absolut. Und ich meine, warum soll man nicht über das, was an

753   Ressourcen frei wird, in Zukunft nutzen, um unser Pflegeproblem zu lösen. Hier könnten

754   zum Beispiel Roboter helfen, die Pflege zu übernehmen.

755

756   00:54:09

757   **Sina Kiene:** Ja, genau. Oder man nutzt die Nische, um mehr Ärzte in Zusammenarbeit

758   mit der KI auszubilden.

759

760   00:54:13

761   **Michael Dehm:** Absolut. Man kann viel daraus machen, wenn man es richtig macht und

762   die Hoffnung stirbt zuletzt.

763

764   00:54:24

765   **Sina Kiene:** Vielen Dank noch einmal für Ihre Zeit. Ich wünsche Ihnen schöne

766   Weihnachten und einen guten Rutsch in das neue Jahr.

767

768   00:54:28

769   **Michael Dehm:** Das wünsche ich Ihnen auch. Viel Erfolg und lassen Sie mich gerne mal

770   wissen, was am Ende daraus geworden ist.

11.4 Appendix D: Interview 2 with Nicoletta Blaschke

1   00:00:00

2   **Sina Kiene:** Hallo, Frau Blaschke.

3

4   00:00:01

5   **Nicoletta Blaschke:** Hallo, Frau Kiene. Ich entschuldige mich schon einmal für meine

6   Stimme. Ich hoffe, dass sie hält, aber ich kämpfe leider mit einer fiesen Erkältung. Ich

7   habe hier aber einen großen Tee stehen.

8

9   00:00:15

10   **Sina Kiene:** Ja, Tee hilft immer. Aber schon mal vielen, vielen Dank dass Sie sich die

11   Zeit heute für mich nehmen, das hilft mir echt enorm.

12

13   00:00:24

14   **Nicoletta Blaschke:** Bin zwar gerade von meiner Kollegin beschimpft worden, weil der

15   Jahresabschluss immer näher rückt. Ich habe Sie ja schon einmal verschoben, deshalb

16   mache ich das Interview heute gerne mit Ihnen.

17

18   00:00:34

19   **Sina Kiene**: Für die Abgabe der Bachelorarbeit habe ich leider auch eine Deadline.

20

21   00:00:45

22   **Nicoletta Blaschke:** Wann müssen Sie abgeben?

23

24   00:00:46

25   **Sina Kiene:** Am 29. Januar 2020.

26

27   00:00:47

28   **Nicoletta Blaschke:** Oh wow, dann tickt aber auch die Uhr.

29

30   00:00:50

31   **Sina Kiene:** Ein bisschen, ein bisschen.

32

33 00:00:52

34 **Nicoletta Blaschke:** Und dann schon entschieden, wo es hingeht?

35

36 00:00:56

37 **Sina Kiene:** Noch nicht wirklich, nein. Noch so in der Schwebe. Mal gucken, vielleicht

38 bleibe ich hier in Hamburg, vielleicht bin ich woanders, vielleicht mache ich noch einen

39 Master.

40

41 00:01:05

42 **Nicoletta Blaschke:** Einen Master würde ich Ihnen empfehlen. Ich sage mal so lange die

43 Zeitspanne zwischen Bachelor und Master nicht zu groß ist, ist es auch noch leichter. Ich

44 habe ein paar bei mir im Team, die jetzt auch den Master noch dranhängen oder schon

45 mittendrin sind, das ist super. Vielleicht mal mit der Mia Hackenberg reden. Die ist gerade

46 der neuste Zugang hier in Hamburg und die ist seit September, glaube ich, offiziell neuer

47 Junior Account Manager bei mir. Und ihr finanzieren wir auch irgendwie das

48 Masterstudium noch und das funktioniert wunderbar.

49

50 00:01:42

51 **Sina Kiene:** Da werde ich mich mal mit ihr in Verbindung setzen. Konnten Sie sich ein

52 bisschen einlesen in das Thema oder die Fragen ansehen?

53

54 00:01:54

55 **Nicoletta Blaschke:** Die Fragen habe ich mir angesehen. Ich hoffe, ich kann zu den

56 meisten Sachen etwas sagen oder zumindest habe ich eine Meinung. Aber das, was Sie

57 mir ursprünglich geschickt haben, habe ich noch nicht geschafft zu lesen. Deswegen: wir

58 gucken wir, wie weit wir kommen.

59

60 00:02:09

61 **Sina Kiene:** Ja, alles gut. Gar kein Problem. Die eigene Meinung ist sowieso immer

62 besser, als die Vorgeprägte von anderen. Dann steigen wir einfach direkt ein mit der

63 ersten Frage: Wie ist Ihre allgemeine Haltung zur KI im alltäglichen Leben?

64

65

66

67   00:02:25

68   **Nicoletta Blaschke:** Sehr, sehr offen. Ich freue mich darauf. Solange
69   datenschutzrechtliche Sachen eingehalten werden. Ich glaube da sind wir in Deutschland
70   ja eher so, ich sage mal nicht das innovativste Land, sondern eher sehr konservativ, sehe
71   ich dem Ganzen sehr positiv/stehe ich dem Ganzen sehr positiv gegenüber.

72

73   00:02:42

74   **Sina Kiene:** Perfekt. Haben Sie denn schon mal Berührungspunkte mit einer KI gehabt
75   und wenn ja, wie waren Ihre Erfahrungen?

76

77   00:02:49

78   **Nicoletta Blaschke:** Ich hatte Berührungen mit KI. Ich war kürzlich im Aon Center of
79   Excellence in Krakau. Das ist ja so das Innovations- und Data-Analytics-Zentrum oder
80   eines von denen von Aon. Wir planen Sachen dorthin outzusourcen und dort wurden mir
81   Vorgänge gezeigt, dass die KI im Prinzip lernt, wie ein normaler Mitarbeiter mit
82   verschiedenen Programmen, mit verschiedenen Schnittstellen arbeitet. Es wurde ein
83   ganzer Arbeitsvorgang gezeigt. Da was rauskopiert, da was Öffnen, da reinkopieren, dann
84   die Suchfunktion starten, das Ergebnis wieder in einer anderen Geschichte kopieren. Es
85   war wie, als wenn man einem Mitarbeiter über die Schulter schaut, nur das der halt
86   schneller und ohne Fehler arbeitet. Fantastisch. Wir haben alle dagestanden: Oh mein
87   Gott! Da habe ich gleich gesehen, wie es auch in der Aon Welt aussehen kann. Ansonsten
88   denke ich bei KI auch noch an Auto, Smart Home. Ich bin mit einem ITler verheiratet. Es
89   gibt diverse Sachen in unserem Haus, die ich nicht mehr alleine bedienen kann, die
90   irgendwie so programmiert wurden, dass sobald ich im Haus bin und das Haus kapiert,
91   dass mein Handy da ist, automatisch irgendwie eine Rollladen-Schaltung startet oder das
92   Licht angeht.

93

94   00:04:08

95   **Sina Kiene:** Erleichtert das Leben.

96

97   00:04:09

98   **Nicoletta Blaschke:** Erleichtert das Leben, manchmal denkt man so: huch, ich habe doch
99   gar nichts gemacht, aber da gewöhnt man sich dran.

100

101   00:04:16

102   **Sina Kiene:** Ich finde es auch sehr interessant, wie sich das in alle Richtungen entwickelt.

103   Es entwickelt sich ja in total verschiedene Richtungen. Mit den Autos oder auch mit der

104   Kriminalitätsprävention. Ich würde jetzt einfach mal behaupten, dass es so die nächste

105   große Erfindung der Menschheit nach den Handys ist. Ich meine, das hat uns ja echt

106   mobiler gemacht und über die ganze Welt connected.

107

108   00:04:37

109   **Nicoletta Blaschke:** Es würde uns auch sicherer machen. Weil ich meine, wenn man jetzt

110   bei Mobilität bleibt, die Autos, die automatisch bremsen, bloß weil sie irgendwie einen

111   Gegenstand erkennen und so weiter. Insgesamt hat es einen positiven Einfluss. Natürlich

112   muss man es kontrollieren können. Aber ich bin optimistisch. Beim Handy dachte ich

113   auch am Anfang erst - braucht niemand aber hat sich schnell geändert.

114

115   00:05:03

116   **Sina Kiene:** Das bewegt ja auch alles immer viel schneller, wenn man zurückdenkt

117   Industrialisierung, das hat bestimmt 300 - 400 Jahre gedauert. Und jetzt mit der Technik

118   von einem Jahrzehnt ins nächste wurden so große Schritte gemacht.

119

120   00:05:16

121   **Nicoletta Blaschke:** Ja, das potenziert sich ja. Diese Zyklen werden ja immer schneller.

122   Ich habe mal irgendwo eine Studie gesehen, wie sich die Größe von Prozessoren

123   verkleinert hat, aber die Kapazität jedes Mal verdoppelt oder verdreifacht hat. Und ich

124   glaube in einer ähnlichen Geschwindigkeit passiert das dann jetzt auch mit der KI. Das

125   Potenzial skaliert halt ganz groß.

126

127   00:05:43

128   **Sina Kiene:** Ich bin mal gespannt, ob die Menschheit dafür bereit ist.

129

130   00:05:46

131   **Nicoletta Blaschke**: Ja, ich glaube mal sie ist bereit. Über manche Sachen werden wir

132   überrascht sein, das können wir jetzt noch nicht sehen, aber aufhalten kann man es

133   sowieso nicht mehr, es hat schon angefangen. Dazu ist man immer zu neugierig und will

134   immer höher, schneller, weiter. Vor allem, wenn es etwas Besseres gibt. Apple Watch ist

135 genauo ein Beispiel. Die misst jetzt irgendwie die Heart Rate, die weiß wann man

136 irgendwie aufgeregt ist, sagt wie man atmen muss und so weiter. Da ist schon so viel, was

137 wir mittlerweile gar nicht als KI mehr sehen, sondern es einfach als selbstverständlich

138 ansehen, was alles neu ist. Deswegen wird es so weitergehen.

139

140 00:06:28

141 **Sina Kiene:** Wie gesagt, ich bin sehr gespannt im Hinblick, wie schnell alles

142 voranschreitet. Ich meine, es gibt ja auch immer mehr Möglichkeiten KI im alltäglichen

143 Leben mit einzubringen, mit den Smart Homes, wie Sie das zu Hause haben und auch mit

144 den Autos. Wo glauben Sie, dass die KI so als größte Innovation den Markt beeinflussen

145 wird?

146

147 00:06:47

148 **Nicoletta Blaschke:** Gute Frage. Also, ich denke mal im Gesundheitssektor auf jeden

149 Fall. Ich sehe zum Beispiel große Fortschritte in der Radiologie, weil man der KI

150 beibringen kann, Röntgenbilder zu lesen und Krebsfrüherkennung zu verbessern. Das

151 wird nie die ausschließliche Maßnahme sein, aber die KI ist viel schneller und sehr, sehr

152 viel präzise, als das menschliche Auge und die menschliche Tagesform. Und ich sage

153 mal, wenn eine KI etwas entdeckt, das dann nur noch mit einem Testbefund zu bestätigen,

154 das ist was viel treffsichereres, als das was heute passiert. Da könnte man mehr Patienten

155 durchschleusen und einfach insgesamt Menschen etwas positives geben. Denn Krebs ist

156 nun mal immer noch da, das ist noch nicht kuriert. Dafür gibt's noch keine KI. Aber die

157 Erkennung zum Beispiel und allgemein die Radiologie, also im Medizinwesen auf jeden

158 Fall. Dann Mobilität. Ganz klar, autonomes Fahren. Das wird kommen, das wird noch

159 viel krasser als jetzt und nicht nur was die Autos angeht. Das wird auch den öffentlichen

160 Nahverkehr betreffen. Das wird auf jeden Fall kommen, aber im Prinzip, alles was sich

161 berechnen lässt, was standardisiert oder was repetierbar ist. Das hat Potenzial für KI. Oder

162 jetzt im Haushalt unsere neue Waschmaschine. Der muss man nichts mehr sagen, die

163 wiegt die Wäsche, die bestimmt den Verschmutzungsgrad und zieht sich dann selbst

164 wieviel Waschmittel sie braucht.

165

166 00:08:21

167 **Sina Kiene:** Was ist das für eine Waschmaschine?

168

169 00:08:24

170 **Nicoletta Blaschke:** Eine Miele. Das Lustige ist, die schickt mir noch irgendwie eine

171 Nachricht aufs Handy und sagt, wenn sie fertig ist. Also ich muss gar nicht mehr selbst

172 in den Keller gehen und gucken. Oder auch Bewässerung, überhaupt Landschaftspflege.

173 Die KI kann genau messen wie der pH-Wert vom Boden ist, wie die Feuchtigkeit ist und

174 dementsprechend kann man Dünge- und Bewässerung steuern. Das muss alles nicht mehr

175 von Menschenhand gemacht werden. Es muss kontrolliert werden, aber es muss nicht

176 mehr selbst gemacht werden. Also ich glaube, was das körperliche Arbeiten angeht und

177 was die Verarbeitung von Daten angeht, da sehe ich die größten Fortschritte in Zukunft.

178

179 00:09:07

180 **Sina Kiene:** Und denken Sie, dass die Daten oder das Datensammeln eine Schattenseite

181 der KI sein wird bzw. die Menschen das als negative Seite ansehen und sich Gedanken

182 darüber machen werden?

183

184 00:09:18

185 **Nicoletta Blaschke:** Absolut. Zumindest in Deutschland. In anderen Ländern sind wir

186 ein bisschen offener, aber ich sage mal bei uns wird es schwierig sein. Man hat ja jetzt

187 schon irgendwie Probleme, wenn einem bewusst ist, was Facebook alles über mich weiß,

188 was Apple alles über mich weiß. Die Bedenken werden da sein, halten uns aber nicht

189 davon ab, diese ganzen Dinge zu nutzen, weil wenn die da sind, werden sie auch genutzt

190 und da wird die Forschung das vorantreiben. Auch die Verfügbarkeit von neuen Features

191 wird das vorantreiben, auch wenn man die Bedenken hat, aber ich sage mal, da ist die

192 Menschheit einfach zu manipulierbar und nicht konsequent. Jetzt haben wir auch schon

193 die Bedenken und alles funktioniert trotzdem. Da ist sich halt der Mensch immer selbst

194 der Nächste, genauso was die Verantwortung angeht. Ja man sollte vielleicht kein iPhone

195 von Apple haben, weil man weiß, dass die Rohstoffe irgendwie durch Kinderarbeit

196 gewonnen werden, das ist alles transparent und verfügbar dieses Wissen. Es hat aber keine

197 Konsequenz, weil der Drang, manche Sachen zu besitzen, einfach stärker ist.

198

199 00:10:21

200 **Sina Kiene:** Einfach diese Angst etwas zu vermissen oder nicht Teil der Gesellschaft zu

201 sein spielt, wie Sie schon sagen, auch immer eine große Rolle.

202

203   00:10:27

204   **Nicoletta Blaschke:** Genau. Und was ich wirklich glaube, jetzt wo ich länger darüber

205   nachdenke, im Gesundheitswesen war ich am Anfang schon. Wir haben unheimlich

206   Probleme in der Pflege. Die Menschheit wird immer älter. Zumindest in den westlichen

207   Industriestaaten wird die Menschheit älter und nicht genügend Jjüngere kommen nach.

208   Das heißt, wir sprechen seit Jahren über einen Pflegenotstand, der noch schlimmer

209   werden wird. Dort in dem Bereich, wird man glaube ich Robotics einbeziehen und da

210   braucht man dann KI. Wenn jemand gehoben werden muss, umgelegt werden muss, keine

211   Ahnung was man sonst noch damit machen kann. Aber das wird definitiv weitergehen

212   und das ist auch gewollt. Da macht sich keiner irgendwelche Gedanken um Datenschutz.

213

214   00:11:11

215   **Sina Kiene:** Da spielt dann auch die Bequemlichkeit der Menschen mit rein.

216

217   00:11:14

218   **Nicoletta Blaschke:** Ja und die Not. Man sagt okay, was ist denn die Alternative. Die

219   Alternative ist niemanden zu haben oder sehr, sehr, sehr, sehr viel Geld für irgendwelche

220   Pflegeheime auszugeben. Aber das ist eine Spirale nach oben. Die Pflegesituation ist nicht

221   gelöst und je eher man dort mit nicht menschlicher Hilfe arbeiten kann, umso besser.

222

223   00:11:37

224   **Sina Kiene:** Wenn man jetzt nochmal auf die KI's und den Gesundheitssektor eingeht.

225   Es gibt ja auch schon Gesichtserkennung und Spracherkennung, die schon Emotionen

226   lesen können. Man kann sagen, ob derjenige traurig ist, allein aus der Sprache und mit

227   dem Gesicht. Glauben Sie, dass es auch später in der Depressionsprävention oder der

228   Diagnostik helfen kann?

229

230   00:11:59

231   **Nicoletta Blaschke:** Da muss ich einfach sagen, ich kann es mir tatsächlich nicht

232   vorstellen. Zumindest die ersten Sachen, die ich gesehen habe, wie die funktionieren. Erst

233   mal bei nicht trainierten Menschen bestimmt, aber wenn ich mich jetzt als Beispiel

234   nehme. Ich habe gelernt in der Arbeitswelt für manche Dinge einfach ein Pokerface

235   aufzusetzen, das heißt Gesichtserkennung würde schon mal nicht so gut funktionieren.

236   Stimmtraining. Jeder Manager muss irgendwann in seinem Leben in ein Stimmtraining.

237 Wie spreche ich, in welcher Lautstärke. Ob man es dann immer anwendet, weiß man
238 nicht. Aber ich glaube nicht, dass die KI so zuverlässig ist, dass sie wirklich zeigen kann,
239 okay der hat eine Depression und ist sich aber nicht bewusst darüber. Da weiß ich aber
240 zu wenig.

241

242 00:12:49

243 **Sina Kiene:** Glauben Sie auch nicht, dass das funktioniert. Ich meine ja teilweise, wenn
244 man jemanden anguckt, den man gerne mag, dann erweitern sich die Pupillen, da kann
245 man ja gar nichts gegen machen. Also so rein biologisch. Ich weiß auch nicht, wie das
246 bei einer Depression ist, ob sich da etwas in der Iris tut, aber das wäre ja tatsächlich auch
247 eine Möglichkeit, die man nicht unterdrücken könnte.

248

249 00:13:09

250 **Nicoletta Blaschke:** Nein, das nicht. Ich glaube, bis zu einem gewissen Grad kann man
251 das machen, aber ich weiß nicht inwieweit das helfen sollte. Ich glaube das, wenn es jetzt
252 meinetwegen Tools gäbe, das zu analysieren - ist bestimmt ein Markt da, aber der Nutzen
253 davon ist für mich noch nicht so greifbar. Das geht dann eher so in Richtung
254 Überwachung. Ich glaube, das wäre wieder negativ belegt. Der Mensch ist zwar sehr
255 offen Daten zu teilen und so weiter, aber wenn er dieses nicht mehr kontrollieren kann,
256 dass so was Persönliches ausgelesen wird - ich glaube da ist so eine Grenze. Das kann ich
257 mir vorstellen, dass das irgendwie Widerstände gibt.

258

259 00:13:57

260 **Sina Kiene:** Zum Beispiel in den USA gibt es schon eine Firma die heißt Beyond Verbal.
261 Die hat eine App für Handys entwickelt und trackt sozusagen die ganze Zeit die Sprache.
262 Dadurch hat die App die Möglichkeit Herzinfarkte oder Emotions zu lesen und zu
263 erkennen. Inzwischen hat die App schon einige Herzinfarkte hervorgesehen, so dass dann
264 präventiv Maßnahmen ergriffen werden konnten. Zum Beispiel Ernährungsumstellung
265 und ähnliches. Wie gesagt, ich weiß nicht, ob das jetzt an der europäischen Kultur liegt,
266 weil wir relativ konservativ mit unseren Daten umgehen. In den USA ist es das Umgehen
267 mit Daten offener und in China erst recht. Diese Länder haben mehr oder weniger keine
268 Wahl. Glauben Sie, dass die Menschen das dann auch proaktiv mit in ihren Alltag
269 integrieren werden?

270

271   00:14:52

272   **Nicoletta Blaschke:** Nein, ich glaube das lässt sich nicht aufrechterhalten. Ich persönlich

273   finde das auch ganz gruselig in China. Die haben ja gar keine Wahl und wenn man weiß,

274   wenn ich in diesem Areal bin, da gibt's irgendwie Kameras, dann kann man auch ab und

275   zu daran denken. Allerdings kann sich der Mensch nicht dauerhaft verstellen. Deshalb

276   kann ich mir nicht vorstellen, dass sich das in der westlichen Welt durchsetzt.

277

278   00:15:19

279   **Sina Kiene:** Da glauben Sie da sind zu viele Hemmungen mit Datenschutz und

280   Überwachungsängsten?

281

282   00:15:22

283   **Nicoletta Blaschke:** Und auch Treffsicherheit. Da müsste ich erstmal sehen, dass das

284   wirklich funktioniert. Auf diese Dinge, die Sie gerade von den USA von diesem Anbieter

285   erzählt haben, also Kopf sagt, das kann doch gar nicht sein und so genau kann man das

286   doch gar nicht sehen, aber vielleicht habe ich halt einfach auch Unrecht. Ich weiß es nicht.

287

288   00:15:55

289   **Sina Kiene:** Es wurde ja auch noch nicht viel in diese Richtung geforscht. Angenommen,

290   die KI würde jetzt so funktionieren und man würde gesetzliche Richtlinien in Deutschland

291   verabschieden und sagen: Wir versichern der Bevölkerung, dass die Daten nur für die

292   Gesundheit verwendet werden und nicht für manipulative Zwecke im Marketing oder

293   nicht für Zwecke anderer Firmen. Glauben Sie, dass das möglich wäre?

294

295   00:16:32

296   **Nicoletta Blaschke:** Nein. Nicht in den nächsten Jahren, das kann ich mir nicht

297   vorstellen. Das ist nicht die Mentalität von Deutschland. Nein, ich glaube da gibt es zu

298   viel Verbraucherschutz und Datenschutz, zu viele Hürden, die man nehmen müsste. Also

299   wenn sowas sich durchsetzt, dann glaube ich eher, dass die Treiber irgendwie aus China

300   oder den USA kommen. Ich sage mal, wenn es mehr gibt, die damit arbeiten, dann wird

301   auch irgendwann Deutschland nachziehen, aber ich glaube das wird noch sehr, sehr lange

302   dauern.

303

304

305   00:17:06

306   **Sina Kiene:** Okay, ich meine, Deutschland ist ja eigentlich immer so ein bisschen am
307   Hinterherhinken was die Technologien angeht, gar keine Frage.

308

309   00:17:14

310   **Nicoletta Blaschke:** Aber dafür ist der Persönlichkeitsschutz in Deutschland sehr hoch,
311   viel höher als in anderen Ländern. Und ich glaube technische Innovationen, auch da ist
312   Deutschland langsam, aber Persönlichkeitsschutz, ich glaube, das ist noch eine viel
313   größere Hürde.

314

315   00:17:30

316   **Sina Kiene:** Da müsste man die Menschen über mehrere Jahre wirklich darauf
317   vorbereiten. Oder was glauben Sie?

318

319   00:17:39

320   **Nicoletta Blaschke:** Man müsste erst die Erfahrung machen, dass das nichts Schlechtes
321   ist. Momentan wird es als etwas Schlechtes gesehen, außer wenn man diese
322   Ausbildungsmöglichkeiten jetzt zum Beispiel nur beim Arzt im Gespräch hätte. Dass der
323   Arzt das als zusätzliche Unterstützung nehmen würde - die KI sagt aber sie haben das,
324   das, das. Haben Sie da schon was gemerkt? - Dass man da gezielter nachfragen kann.
325   Aber das zum Beispiel das Smart Home einen überwachen würde und die Atmung
326   überwachen würde und dann sagen würde - Achtung du bist gefährdet, dass so etwas
327   passiert - ne irgendwie ist das für mich noch zu weit weg für Deutschland.

328

329   00:18:21

330   **Sina Kiene:** Noch zu Science-Fiction?

331

332   00:18:22

333   **Nicoletta Blaschke:** Ja, genau. Irgendwie glaube ich nicht, wenn ich sehe, dass bei
334   einfacheren Sachen schon die Widerstände so groß sind, dass es sich noch nicht so schnell
335   durchsetzen lassen wird. Aber wie gesagt, es geht immer darum, hat die Gesellschaft mal
336   Vertrauen geschöpft, entweder, weil sie es in anderen Ländern gesehen hat, dann läuft die
337   Maschinerie. Aber dieses Vertrauen erst zu gewinnen, das ist die größte Hürde für eine
338   Technologieentwicklung.

339   00:18:51

340   **Sina Kiene:** Das heißt, es muss erst mal positive Case Studies sozusagen geben, die auf

341   den Markt gebracht werden, um das Tool sozusagen zu verkaufen.

342

343   00:18:59

344   **Nicoletta Blaschke:** Da muss aber auch viel kommuniziert werden. Viel Transparenz und

345   die dürfen sich keine Fehler erlauben, weil, das ist halt immer die Gefahr, wenn man

346   Zweifel hat und dann denkt, man ich versuch langsam zu vertrauen - wenn dann

347   irgendetwas Negatives rauskommt, irgendwie Datenmissbrauch oder irgendetwas, was

348   da schiefgelaufen ist, dann ist es auch wieder schwierig. Dann wirft es die KI wieder ein

349   paar Jahre zurück. Aber Deutschland braucht Vertrauen.

350

351   00:19:27

352   **Sina Kiene:** Ich meine jetzt zum Beispiel Alexa oder Amazon, die sammeln ja total viele

353   Daten auch von unserer Seite. Also von unserem Kaufverhalten. Auf den Internetseiten

354   verweisen sie dann ja auch immer wieder auf passende Produkte aus ihren Produktionen.

355   Das ist ja auch eine Art von Manipulation.

356

357   00:19:42

358   **Nicoletta Blaschke:** Absolut. Und auch das. Die Leute wissen das und sie machen es

359   trotzdem, weil sie auf die Alexa nicht mehr verzichten wollen. Das ist so. Dieser

360   Zwiespalt. Einerseits sagt man, na ja ich sage nichts Vertrauliches, aber nicht, wenn so

361   was rauskommt, dass man aus der Stimme und so weiter schon viel mehr auslesen kann,

362   als man eigentlich sagt. Dann gibt man auch über Alexa von der Persönlichkeit mehr preis

363   oder wie auch immer die Tools heißen. Das ist tatsächlich bei mir auch noch so eine

364   Barriere. Sowas haben wir nicht zuhause. Alles andere, aber wir haben keine Alexa oder

365   kein Homepot oder so. Ich denke mal, das Telefon hört sowieso mit, weil wenn ich "hey

366   Siri" sage, sie ja auch antworte. Wahrscheinlich mache ich mir was vor, was ich denke,

367   dass ich da noch eine Barriere habe. Aber bewusst würde ich das jetzt nicht eingehen

368   wollen.

369

370

371

372

373   00:20:45

374   **Sina Kiene:** Sie haben schon erwähnt, dass das Licht in ihrem Haus über Ihr Handy

375   gesteuert wird. Können Sie sich dann nicht auch vorstellen, dass Alexa diesen Part

376   übernimmt?

377

378   00:20:58

379   **Nicoletta Blaschke:** Das würde wunderbar mit sowas funktionieren. Ja, vielleicht kaufe

380   ich mir Alexa auch irgendwann. Ich glaube schon, dass es irgendwann so ist, dass man

381   sagt: "Wie, du hast keine Alexa?" Jetzt warte ich persönlich lieber noch, da es noch ein

382   bisschen getestet wird und bis ich dann vielleicht irgendwann nicht mehr nein sagen kann.

383   Und dann auch eine habe. Ich weiß es nicht.

384

385   00:21:22

386   **Sina Kiene:** Sie meinen, dass Alexa später wahrscheinlich so in die Gesellschaft etabliert

387   wird, wie Handys damals.?

388

389   00:21:28

390   **Nicoletta Blaschke:** Ganz genau.

391

392   00:21:31

393   **Sina Kiene:** Sehr interessant. Ich hatte ja mit ihrem Kollegen Herrn Dehm gestern

394   telefoniert. Der ging total in die andere Richtung.

395

396   00:21:39

397   **Nicoletta Blaschke:** Hätte ich jetzt wetten können. Er ist jetzt nicht viel älter als ich, aber

398   er ist trotzdem noch eine andere Generation.

399

400   00:21:48

401   **Sina Kiene:** Ich finde es total interessant so unterschiedliche Meinungen zu hören, weil

402   innerhalb meiner Bachelor-Arbeit beide bzw. unterschiedliche Seiten aufzeigt werden.

403

404

405

406

407   00:21:57

408   **Nicoletta Blaschke:** Ja, auf jeden Fall und das ist ja genau das Bild. Ich finde das Thema

409   sehr interessant. Ich weiß, dass ich darüber an Weihnachten spreche, wenn ich mit meiner

410   Schwester zusammen bin. Sie hat Familie, zwei Kinder. Bei denen ist nichts digital

411   verknüpft oder so. Die haben noch für jedes Gerät eine einzelne Fernbedienung und so

412   weiter. Die würden nie was mit dem Handy als remote steuern. Und wenn ich solche

413   Fragen stelle, dann weiß ich, dass ich ganz genau ein krasses „Nein" zur Antwort erhalte.

414

415   00:22:31

416   **Sina Kiene:** Was aber interessant ist, vor allem Kinder werden ja auch in der Schule und

417   von Freunden stark beeinflusst, die von ihren Eltern die Technologien kennen oder selber

418   welche haben.

419

420   00:22:40

421   **Nicoletta Blaschke:** Aber die sind eher Treiber. Also meine kleinen Nichten, die eine ist

422   jetzt 12, haben beide schon ein Smartphone. Es ist aber nicht so, dass die Eltern das

423   unbedingt wollten, sondern weil einfach der Terror zu groß war und weil alle anderen in

424   der Schule das hatten. Das heißt, die werden viel eher offen sein für Neues. Da muss man

425   eher aufpassen, dass sie nicht alles teilen und da sehr sensibel mit den Daten umgehen,

426   aber für die ist das ganz normal. Die werden groß mit Familien die Alexa haben, die

427   können sich das gar nicht anders vorstellen, dass man noch selbst irgendwo hinlaufen

428   muss und Sachen selbst z.B. einkaufen gehen muss. Und die werden das dann treiben.

429

430   00:23:14

431   **Sina Kiene:** Glauben Sie, dass es nicht wirklich einen Generationskonflikt gibt? Ich

432   meine, es gibt ja auch welche aus der anderen Generation, die KI total befürworten. Mein

433   Großonkel, der liebt das, der hat alles was es gibt, gefühlt. Glauben Sie, dass es dann eher

434   so an Vertrauen und Persönlichkeit liegt?

435

436   00:23:32

437   **Nicoletta Blaschke:** Ja, das Handy ist ja auch kein Generationenproblem mehr. Heute

438   haben auch die Senioren, selbst meine Eltern die haben Smartphones. Es gehört einfach

439   dazu. Navigationssysteme, früher auch total überflüssig. Da hat man sich gebrüstet, wenn

440   man die Wege noch auswendig konnte. Das ist halt heute einfach alles nicht mehr

441 notwendig und das hat mit der Generation nichts mehr zu tun. Bei digital sind wir jetzt
442 alle offener, egal ob irgendwie frühere Generationen oder heutige Generationen. Es ist
443 eher was mit Neugierde und Weltoffenheit. Aber ich glaube, man kann es eher in
444 politische Lager sogar noch unterteilen. Ich sage mal, die sehr konservativ und rechts
445 wählen, sind jetzt wahrscheinlich nicht die KI-freundlichsten.
446
447 00:24:26
448 **Sina Kiene:** Da haben Sie recht, dass es einfach auch an den Demographiken
449 festzumachen ist.
450
451 00:24:33
452 **Nicoletta Blaschke:** Oder Bildungsstand. Jemand mit einem akademischen Abschluss,
453 der schon viele Länder bereist hat oder auch Ihre Generation, da wird ein Studium
454 gemacht, ein Auslandsaufenthalt ist quasi normal, das war früher ein großes Ereignis.
455 Man wird neugieriger und schaut nicht mehr nur hier auf den eigenen Tisch und guckt
456 einfach was in der Welt passiert. Leute die das tun, ich glaube, die sind auch die Treiber
457 von diesen ganzen Innovationen, denn die wissen ganz genau: "oh guck mal da in den
458 USA. Mal gucken, wann es endlich in Deutschland ankommt" und die werden das treiben.
459 Aber nicht die, die daran festhalten "Früher war alles besser und ich möchte gar keine
460 Veränderung."
461
462 00:25:16
463 **Sina Kiene:** Das hält ja auch die Evolution zurück.
464
465 00:25:20
466 **Nicoletta Blaschke:** Ja, ganz genau. Aber an dem Geburtsjahrgang kann man es nicht
467 festmachen.
468
469 00:25:28
470 **Sina Kiene:** Ich glaube, dann haben wir alles von den Fragen abgedeckt. Ich habe nicht
471 alle gestellt, aber Sie haben schon so viele beantwortet, sodass ich nicht mehr nachhaken
472 muss.
473
474

475   00:25:41

476   **Nicoletta Blaschke:** Ich hoffe, es war einigermaßen klar. Also wenn noch irgendetwas

477   ist. Gerne noch mal durchklingeln oder noch mal eine E-Mail schreiben. Ich finde, Sie

478   haben sich ein extrem spannendes Thema für Ihre Bachelorarbeit ausgesucht. Einige

479   Bachelorarbeiten sind auch interessant, aber regen nicht so zum Nachdenken an, wie Ihre.

480   Hier musste ich selbst ein wenig denken, das macht Spaß.

481

482   00:26:06

483   **Sina Kiene:** Das freut mich sehr. Wenn die Leute meine Arbeit gerne lesen., vielleicht

484   wird man dann später einmal darauf angesprochen.

485

486   00:26:17

487   **Nicoletta Blaschke:** Ich würde mich freuen die Bachelorarbeit dann auch mal lesen zu

488   dürfen.

489

490   00:26:20

491   **Sina Kiene:** Ja, sehr gerne. Sobald ich die Interviews mit eingearbeitet habe, schicke ich

492   sie Ihnen gerne einmal zu.

493

494   00:26:24

495   **Nicoletta Blaschke:** Ja, super klasse.

496

497   00:26:27

498   **Sina Kiene:** Dann wünsche ich noch einen schönen Abend und schöne Weihnachten.

499

500   00:26:30

501   **Nicoletta Blaschke:** Danke schön. Das wünsche ich Ihnen ganz genauso. Dann toi, toi,

502   toi und gute Nerven. Ich weiß, eine Bachelor-Arbeit zu schreiben, kostet auch immer

503   irgendwie Kraft. Aber Sie machen das schon.

504

505   00:26:40

506   **Sina Kiene:** Vielen Dank. Einen schönen Abend noch.

507

508

11.5 Appendix E: Interview 3 with Lothar Hotz

1 00:00:00

2 **Sina Kiene:** Perfekt, genau. Soll ich es Ihnen einmal noch kurz erklären, wie weit ich

3 schon mit meiner These bin.

4

5 00:00:08

6 **Lothar Hotz**: Ja, gerne.

7

8 00:00:08

9 **Sina Kiene**: Ich habe mich, wie gesagt darauf fokussiert: Was ist KI? Was steht hinter

10 der Technologie? Welche verschiedenen Prozesse vom Lernen hat die Technologie etc.?

11 Besonders auf den Gesundheitssektor bezogen, ob das jetzt zu Prävention oder Hilfe von

12 Diagnostika beitragen kann, das ist jetzt die Frage - da bin ich noch in der Schwebe, sagen

13 wir es mal so. Ich setze auch den ganz großen Fokus darauf, dass sich die Menschheit

14 oder Generationen darauf einstellen müssen, dass künstliche Intelligenz eine neue Ära ist,

15 die jetzt nach den Smartphones folgt. Jetzt bin ich so in den letzten Zügen. Mir fehlen

16 noch 10 Seiten von meiner Bachelorarbeit und dann ist diese auch fertig. Ich glaube, dann

17 können wir eigentlich auch mit den Fragen einsteigen. Wie ist denn Ihre allgemeine

18 Haltung zur KI im alltäglichen Leben und ihrem privaten Leben?

19

20 00:01:28

21 **Lothar Hotz:** Benutzen tue ich sie nicht bewusst. Letztens hatte ich noch so einen Chat

22 Bot irgendwo, der hat sich auch als solcher geoutet, aber inwiefern dahinter auch KI stand,

23 das weiß man nicht direkt. Selbst wenn er eine Antwort geben kann, muss dahinter jetzt

24 nicht großartig was stehen. Also allenfalls solche Serviceseite, aber zum Beispiel sowas

25 auch wie Text oder Spracherkennung, habe ich nicht benutzt.

26

27 00:01:57

28 **Sina Kiene:** Auch nicht auf Ihrem Handy, mal mit Google Assistant?

29

30 00:02:05

31 **Lothar Hotz:** Also allenfalls den Fingerabdruck hinten auf dem Handy, aber sonst nicht.

32 KI ist halt auch schon ein großer Bereich, der im Machine Learning aktuell ist. Aber es

33   gibt jetzt einen klassischen Bereich, der jetzt auch Suchmaschinen und so beinhaltet oder
34   Symantic-Web - und die benutze ich natürlich schon. Das ist natürlich ein Bereich, den
35   jeder benutzt, Beispiel Google. Da ist das Stichwort Knowledge Graph als semantischer
36   Graph der dahinter steckt, um die Suchanfragen quasi auch auf semantischer Basis zu
37   beantworten. Diese Technologien, die merkt man gar nicht. Aber vielleicht kann man das
38   unterscheiden. Die klassischen Anwendungen sind schon da, die werden jetzt auch nicht
39   in ihrem Sinne vielleicht in den nächsten Jahren irgendetwas ändern an der Stelle. Die
40   werden sich natürlich weiterentwickeln, aber das heißt, wir fokussieren uns jetzt erst mal
41   nur auf den maschinellen Lernbereich. Selbst einen Sprachassistent, habe ich nicht immer
42   am Start sozusagen. Bildverarbeitung habe ich auch im PC durch Gesichtserkennung.
43
44   00:03:34
45   **Sina Kiene:** Bei Ihrer Arbeit haben Sie bestimmt viele Berührungspunkte mit der KI?
46
47   00:03:41
48   **Lothar Hotz:** Ja, da haben wir natürlich Projekte, wo wir ein KI-System entwickeln, um
49   zum Beispiel Stempel zu erkennen auf Formularen. Das ist natürlich jetzt auch indem
50   Sinne intelligent. Die KI muss natürlich finden, wo der Stempel überhaupt ist, um den
51   Bereich dann zu analysieren, dass man womöglich erkennt, von wem dieser Stempel
52   kommt. Die Adresse ist ja meistens im Stempel, sodass viele Leute nicht das Formular
53   ausfüllen. Auch die Analyse von Gesichtern ist ein anderes Projekt, wo wir versuchen
54   Hautflächen zu erkennen. Ein anders Forschungsprojekt: Bei dem geht es darum, wenn
55   man ein Produktionssystem hat - also Maschinenbau-System - z.B. Bleche ausstanzen.
56   Das System benutzt quasi die gesammelten Daten, um die eigene Verwendung somit zu
57   prüfen, zu tracken und abzuspeichern. Durch die Analysen der KI können somit Prozesse
58   optimiert werden. Es lernt quasi durch die Verwendung. Es erkennt mittels Hilfe des
59   Maschine-Learnings, welche Situation denn jetzt gerade vorliegt und verwendet
60   letztendlich klassische KI-Verfahren, um dann heraus zu analysieren, wie es sich ändern
61   muss. Z.B. Suchmaschinenverfahren oder Konfigurierungsverfahren. Das ist eine
62   Kombination von maschinellen Lernen und dem klassischen KI-Verfahren. Also das sind
63   jetzt drei Beispiele. Es gibt noch mehr, aber...
64
65
66

00:06:08

68 **Sina Kiene:** Drei Beispiele sind schon einmal sehr gut! Es wird ja auch echt viel
69 momentan in die Richtung der KI-Systeme geforscht, also wirklich in alle Richtungen -
70 beim Auto oder beim Handy oder jetzt mit Alexa. Ich würde einfach einmal behaupten,
71 dass die KI die nächste große Erfindung nach dem Smartphone ist. Wie stehen Sie zu der
72 Aussage?
73
74 00:06:29
75 **Lothar Hotz:** Das Smartphone ist ja direkt ein Gerät, was jeder Mensch benutzt. Vorher
76 waren es ja Handys und jeder einzelne Mensch hat telefoniert und jetzt haben wir quasi
77 das Smartphone. Deswegen war es meines Erachtens eben diese Revolution, weil viele
78 Menschen das Bedürfnis hatten, zu telefonieren. Sie können jetzt eben auch auf das
79 Internet zugreifen und andere Dinge damit machen. KI ist eher so eine enabeling
80 technology, die bestimmte Anwendungen ermöglicht. Zum Beispiel für Smartphones. Es
81 wird ja jetzt nicht so sein, dass jeder ein Gerät hat, was als KI gilt, sondern es wird
82 vielleicht neue Funktionalitäten im Smartphone ermöglichen, zum Beispiel über den
83 Fingerabdruck.
84
85 00:07:30
86 **Sina Kiene:** Also eine Evolution in dem Bereich der Smart Devices sozusagen?
87
88 00:07:34
89 **Lothar Hotz:** Ja, natürlich nicht nur da, aber da auch. Inwieweit es dann so eine
90 Veränderung hervorbringt, wie die Smartphones, ist fraglich. Da ist es eher so, dass z.B.
91 bei Industrie- und Versicherungen, da wo eben auch viele Daten anfallen, eher zu
92 Änderungen kommen wird. Es ist halt Mustererkennung - heißt es ja auch jetzt - was jetzt
93 neue Anwendungen ermöglicht und das ist halt dann wichtig überall da, wo man Muster
94 in den Daten erkennen kann. Da ist es dann auch sinnvoll, auf Bilder oder Sprache zu
95 achten. Aber das muss man erstmal finden. Ich bin mir nicht sicher, ob das wirklich so
96 krass ist, wie jetzt Smartphones oder so.
97
98
99
100

101 00:08:57

102 **Sina Kiene:** Wahrscheinlich werden dann nicht nur Bereiche wie Industrie- oder
103 Versicherungen sehr stark betroffen sein. Jetzt aber in Richtung Gesundheitssektor, da
104 spielt ja auch ein wenig die Versicherung mit hinein. Z.B. die Krankenversicherung. Wie
105 glauben Sie, könnte die KI damit hineinspielen?

106

107 00:09:15

108 **Lothar Hotz:** Da wird es schon Mustererkennungen geben. Zum Beispiel Bilder oder so.
109 Dieses gibt es ja auch schon für Ärzte oder den diagnostischen Bereich. Da wird quasi
110 die KI sozusagen ein weiteres Werkzeug für den Arzt sein, wo dann das Röntgenbild oder
111 auch Videos in ein KI-System gesteckt wird und das macht dann einen Vorschlag, was
112 eben sein oder nicht sein könnte. So ähnlich gibt es auch andere seriöse statistische
113 Verfahren oder sowas, die ein Arzt vielleicht auch verwendet, wie bisher andere
114 Verfahren. Es wird auf jeden Fall da ein neues Tool für die Diagnose geben und das kann
115 man natürlich dann nicht nur Ärzten, sondern auch Patienten zur Verfügung stellen. Da
116 sind auch schon Diagnostikmethoden in der Therapie. Es gibt ja auch schon Ansätze, dass
117 so kleine Roboterpuppen oder so gebaut werden, die dann eben Kranken gegeben werden,
118 die dann ihrer Therapie helfen und sich damit beschäftigen.

119

120 00:10:32

121 **Sina Kiene:** Wenn wir jetzt auf Deutschland gucken? Deutschland oder Europa
122 allgemein ist relativ konservativ gegenüber neuen Erfindungen - vor allem technologisch
123 – als sagen wir mal China und Amerika. Wobei die Bevölkerung Chinas glaube ich wenig
124 beeinflussen kann, weil die einfach keine Rechte haben, was Daten angeht. Was glauben
125 Sie, sind so die Challenges in Deutschland die man beachten müsste, um eine KI so in
126 einem größeren Bereich zu implementieren?

127

128 00:11:02

129 **Lothar Hotz:** Man muss zunächst mal identifizieren, wo man das wirklich anwenden
130 kann und dann entsprechend die Gelder finden und vor allen Dingen auch die Industrie,
131 kleinere oder größere Firmen dazu motivieren und ihnen ermöglichen, dass sie prüfen
132 können, ob denn KI-Systeme, in ihrem Produktionssystem oder Unternehmen eingesetzt
133 werden können. Das muss also erstmal ermöglicht werden. Wir haben hier ein bisschen
134 andere Vorgaben, die wir erfüllen müssen - im Vergleich zu China zum Beispiel. Das

135 kann natürlich auch erst mal eine Herausforderung sein, aber auch ein positives Merkmal
136 für Europa. Wenn wir das dann berücksichtigen, dann wollen das andere vielleicht auch
137 so machen. Ich denke an der Stelle an diese Datenschutzverordnung. Wenn wir sagen,
138 diese Systeme sind GVO-konform in irgendeiner Art und Weise, gerade im
139 Gesundheitsbereich, dann ist das auch etwas, was die Chinesen eben gar nicht machen,
140 weil die nicht die Vorgaben haben. Man muss natürlich gucken - das ist natürlich ein
141 Zwiespalt - dass die Vorgaben uns in diesem Sinne nicht hindern.
142
143 00:12:38
144 **Sina Kiene:** Also eher vor Cyber Risiken schützen?
145
146 00:12:45
147 **Lothar Hotz:** Also, dass sie die Innovation nicht behindern. So offensichtlich ist es nicht,
148 wie man dieses KI-System GVO-konform machen kann, aber wir probieren es mal mit
149 der Datenschutzrichtlinie. Auch eine Herausforderung. Man kann ja aber schon vieles
150 machen. Die Vorgabe erlaubt ja auch, dass man erst mal hinschreiben muss, was gemacht
151 wird, um eben solche Grenzen setzen zu können.
152
153 00:13:24
154 **Sina Kiene:** Also sozusagen, dass die Gesellschaft genau weiß, was genau mit den Daten
155 passieren wird. Es gibt ja schon KI's z.B. Gesichtserkennung und auch....
156
157 00:13:41
158 **Lothar Hotz:** Man spricht eigentlich immer von KI-Systemen. Ich vermeide, KI zu
159 sagen. Ein Problem ist eben, dass es so eine Art Personifizierung des KI-Systems ist,
160 wenn man nur KI sagt. Es wird sozusagen vermenschlicht und gerade im
161 Gesundheitsbereich ist das quasi positiv oder auch negativ. Es ist eben fragwürdig meines
162 Erachtens, wenn ein Patient - in der Diagnostik nicht so problematisch - mit einem KI-
163 System zusammenkommt und er dann sagt: "Ach, das ist aber niedlich". Dann projiziert
164 der Patient etwas auf das System, was gar nicht da ist.
165
166 00:14:36
167 **Sina Kiene:** Also dürften KI-Systeme Ihrer Meinung nach im Gesundheitssektor nicht
168 vermenschlicht werden, damit es einfach auf einer professionellen Ebene bleibt?

169   00:14:42

170   **Lothar Hotz:** Ja, auf einer Distanz oder das eben klar ist/wird, das ist eine Maschine. Es

171   ist eben nicht glücklich oder es ist nicht niedlich. Der Mensch, der mit dem KI-System

172   interagiert hat die Emotion. Es ist wie bei einer Puppe, die ist auch niedlich, aber das hat

173   man glaube ich begriffen, dass die keine Gefühle hat. Aber die Gefahr besteht halt bei

174   KI-Systemen darin, dass man denkt, die kann ja schon so alleine denken und spricht ja so

175   wie wir. Man muss im Hinterkopf behalten, dass es eine Maschine ist. Auch jeder Patient

176   oder wer auch immer, sollte immer noch einmal mit einem Schild oder etwas Ähnlichem

177   informiert werden: Das ist die KI ein System und kein Mensch.

178

179   00:15:30

180   **Sina Kiene:** Sozusagen ein Hinweis auf die "Nicht-Menschlichkeit". Es gibt ja jetzt auch

181   inzwischen wirklich Systeme - Gesichtserkennung und Spracherkennung - die Emotionen

182   lesen können. Durch Bewegungen am Mundwinkel, die Vergrößerung der Pupillen oder

183   halt durch die Tonalisierung in der Stimme. Glauben Sie, dass die KI-Systeme auch dazu

184   verwendet werden können, z.B. Depressionen zu diagnostizieren?

185

186   00:16:00

187   **Lothar Hotz:** Ich weiß jetzt nicht genau was eine Depression ist. Wenn es so ein System

188   dafür geben würde, dann müsste man zum Beispiel Experten an der Stelle fragen. Es

189   müssten mindestens die Bilder annotiert werden - das ist depressiv, das ist nicht depressiv

190   - und dann müsste man die Genauigkeit definieren. Ich kann mir zum Beispiel vorstellen,

191   dass der Ausdruck von Traurigkeit und der Ausdruck einer Depression gar nicht so im

192   Bild zu sehen ist. Also spontan würde ich sagen, man kann zum Beispiel nicht damit

193   diagnostizieren, dass jemand depressiv ist. Ich kann mir nicht vorstellen, dass

194   Psychologen eine Depression anhand eines Bildes diagnostizieren. Die Frage richtet sich

195   ja auch an einen menschlichen Experten. Die Frage wäre glaube ich, sind Psychologen in

196   der Lage Depression nur an Bildern zu erkennen. Das kann ich mir vorstellen, dass das

197   kein Psychologe unterschreiben kann. Dann würde man ja genau diese ganzen

198   Vorgespräche etc. nicht haben müssen. Ich meine auch, wenn man kommuniziert, sehen

199   wir ihn/sie ja nicht, sondern diese Kombination - sehen & hören - bringt mehr

200   Informationen. Trotzdem kann ich mir das bei der KI gar nicht vorstellen.

201

202

203 00:17:43

204 **Sina Kiene:** Es gibt ja auch eine Firma aus Schweden, die kann zum Beispiel die
205 Augenbewegung tracken und gucken, was spricht einen an, was spricht einen eher nicht
206 an - zum Beispiel im Supermarkt oder in einem Video. Wäre es nicht auch möglich für
207 eine KI Emotionen zu lesen und dann auch zu analysieren?

208

209 00:18:08

210 **Lothar Hotz:** Ja, eine KI kann natürlich wieder Vorschläge machen. Anhand von meinet
211 wegen eines Trackings oder auch an einem Gesicht zum Beispiel: Das wird als fröhlich
212 empfunden. Ich finde, es ist schon ein Unterschied zu sagen, ob jemand dann auch
213 depressiv ist und das hängt dann auch davon ab, wie man die KI natürlich trainiert hat.
214 Zu Anfang wird wahrscheinlich nur eine kleine Anzahl von Klassen gewählt: ängstlich,
215 traurig, seien es 20 oder so - das wäre dann auch ok, um solche Anwendung zu
216 programmieren, dass dann der Roboter genauso das Gesicht verzieht oder dann auch
217 freundlich guckt. Dann also die Emotion spiegelt, das geht dann alles. Es gibt aber da
218 sicher noch Nuancen zwischen. Man kommt damit also schon ein Stück weit, man kann
219 Emotionen erkennen, aber was man damit jetzt macht, das ist noch eine andere Frage.

220

221 00:19:18

222 **Sina Kiene:** Es gibt auch schon eine Firma in Amerika, die heißt Beyond Verbal und die
223 haben eine App: BeyondClinic. Diese App trackt die Stimme, die ganze Zeit in real-time
224 und sendet dann Nachrichten an den Arzt und an die Person selbst, wenn etwas
225 Ungewöhnliches herausgefiltert wird, was eine Krankheit initiieren könnte. Auch mit
226 einer Smartwatch zum Beispiel, wenn die Herzrate unregelmäßig ist, dann geht sofort
227 eine Benachrichtigung an ein Krankenhaus. Glauben Sie, dass es dann auch, sagen wir
228 mal die Reaktionszeit von Ärzten/Krankenhäusern verbessert?

229

230 00:19:55

231 **Lothar Hotz:** Solche Sachen schon. Das sind dann eben diese Vorschläge, von den ich
232 sprach, die das System meldet und diese Muster in der Stimme, wenn diese vibriert oder
233 so, herauszuhören ist. Es gibt hier Krankheiten, die sich wirklich durch ein Muster
234 darstellen lassen, das dann eindeutig ist. Denn depressiv ist schon ein großes Ding. Aber
235 Parkinson, da kann man wahrscheinlich meines Erachtens schon sagen, das ab einem
236 gewissen zittern oder so über eine gewisse Zeit die Diagnostik durch eine KI gemacht

237 werden kann. Da ist natürlich das Merkmal sehr eindeutig. Da kann nicht mehr viel
238 hineininterpretiert werden. Das ist natürlich leichter und schneller. Aber so ein Muster,
239 ein erkanntes Muster, ist irgendwie nur ein Teil der Entscheidung, die dann danach
240 kommt.

241

242 00:21:04

243 **Sina Kiene:** Also physisch sichtbare Krankheiten sind einfacher für die Systeme zu
244 lesen?

245

246 00:21:15

247 **Lothar Hotz:** Ja, genau. Deutlich erkennbare physische Ursachen, wie aber auch zum
248 Beispiel die Stimme.

249

250 00:21:28

251 **Sina Kiene:** Dieses Thema ist wirklich hochinteressant und so weitläufig. Ich könnte
252 noch viel mehr schreiben. Ich bin wirklich traurig, dass ich da auf meine Seitenvorgabe
253 limitiert bin.

254

255 00:21:32

256 **Lothar Hotz:** Die nächste Arbeit kommt bestimmt.

257

258 00:21:41

259 **Sina Kiene:** Genau und dann werde ich das Thema weiterführen. Wenn man jetzt so auf
260 andere Erfindungen z.B. das Smartphone guckt - das hat ja schon seine Zeit gedauert, bis
261 das von der Menschheit auf der größeren Fläche akzeptiert wurde. Wie lange glauben Sie,
262 dass es bei den KI-Systemen dauern könnte, dass man sagt, jedes Haus hat jetzt ein KI-
263 System bei sich stehen?

264

265 00:22:09

266 **Lothar Hotz:** Wie gesagt, da wird ein System enthalten sein. Intelligente
267 Kaffeemaschine oder sowas. Es wird also nicht ein System geben, dass die KI darstellt.
268 Es kann schon sein, dass die Möbel nach und nach anfangen. Z.B. Waschmaschine und
269 Kühlschrank - mehr Datensammeln oder Vorschläge machen. Wir hatten ja schon damals
270 mit einem KI Forschungsprojekt 1987, nämlich genau diese Konfigurierungssysteme.

271 Wenn man heute zum Beispiel ein Auto haben will, dann geht man auf eine Webseite und
272 dort wird man gefragt, was man genau will und das System rechnet dann quasi aus, was
273 auf die Filter passt. Ende der 80er Anfang der 90er bis 95 haben wir an dem Projekt
274 geforscht. 2000 haben wir angefangen, mit einem Unternehmen das Ergebnis dieser
275 Forschung in ein Tool zu gießen. 2005 war das dann fertig - so ein Konfigurator, das heißt
276 da sind schon mal so 10 Jahre vergangen. Ich denke mir mal, dass die KI nach und nach
277 kommen wird. Wir haben ja schon festgestellt, dass ein paar Sachen in Smartphones
278 eingebaut wurden. Sagen wir mal in acht Jahren, dann hat man in vielen Dingen auch ein
279 kleines KI-System drinnen. Ich denke immer ein bisschen an diesen Roboter der da saugt.
280 Das wird wahrscheinlich mit der erste sein, den ich mir anschaffe. Der hat ja auch eine
281 gewisse Intelligenz. Der kann zum Beispiel einen Grundriss aufnehmen. Vielleicht wird
282 der nachher auch noch schlauer oder so. Es ist eben diese Art der
283 Mustererkennungsaufgaben, die dann der eine oder andere macht, z.B. der
284 Fingerabdruck. Es wird wahrscheinlich dann, wenn es soweit ist (5-8 Jahre), keiner mehr
285 wissen, dass das jetzt im Jahr 2020 als KI-System bezeichnet worden ist - das Erkennen
286 des Fingerabdrucks.
287
288 00:25:17
289 **Sina Kiene:** Das ist dann einfach schon wieder so normal für die Menschheit geworden.
290
291 00:25:26
292 **Lothar Hotz:** Ja, genau. Man kann es sich auch so vorstellen: Ganz früher gab es noch
293 keine Datenbanken und da gab es nur Zettel, ganze Keller voller Akten. Das dauert ja
294 immer noch an... Andererseits wäre es auch nicht verwunderlich, die Notwendigkeit einer
295 Datenbank zu normalisieren.
296
297 00:26:07
298 **Sina Kiene:** Die Akzeptanz im Sinne von Data Privacy - da haben wir ja schon drüber
299 gesprochen. Wenn es ein Angriff geben würde, z.B. auf sagen wir die Gesundheitsdaten
300 und es werden welche gezogen. Was wären präventive Maßnahmen oder was könnte man
301 mit den KI-Systemen machen, um das zu verhindern? Gibt es überhaupt diese
302 Möglichkeiten?
303
304

305   00:26:37

306   **Lothar Hotz:** Zum Beispiel die Daten zu sichern und sicher abzufangen, das ist

307   sozusagen ein anderes Gebiet nämlich Cybersecurity. Die forschen, wie man eigentlich

308   Daten sichern kann. Das ist an sich kein KI-Gebiet, aber in der Regel gibt es Verfahren

309   der Anonymisierung oder der Dezentralisierung. Stichwort Blockchain, so könnte man

310   eine gewisse Sicherheit erlangen. So könnte man vielleicht auch Gesundheitsdaten

311   verarbeiten und abspeichern. Um ein KI-System mit diesen Daten zum Beispiel etwas tun

312   zu lassen, müssen diese dann auch wieder decodiert werden. Wenn die Daten

313   verschlüsselt worden sind, müssen die erst mal wieder herausgeholt werden. Das sind erst

314   mal so zwei Gebiete. Also die Frage nach: Wie sicher ist das? Da würde man jetzt einfach

315   Security Methoden verwenden und da gibt es auch gerade in der Gesundheit viele

316   Anstrebungen, es möglichst zu anonymisieren. Ein bisschen muss man da immer

317   aufpassen, da Namen oder Adresse herausgenommen werden müssen, sodass man nur

318   mit wenigen Merkmalen - man hat ja für jede Person gewisse Merkmale - diese Person

319   identifizieren kann. Die eine Frau, die hier in Stelling wohnt, man weiß nicht wo genau,

320   aber es ist auf jeden Fall eine Frau und man weiß das ungefähre Alter etc. Da kann man

321   schon sagen: Das kann eigentlich nur die sein. Auf sowas muss man quasi achten, wenn

322   mit Daten gearbeitet wird.

323

324   00:28:53

325   **Sina Kiene:** Das heißt Firmen im Gesundheitssektor müssten mit anderen

326   Versicherungsfirmen zusammenarbeiten, um Cyber-Risiko-Lösungen zu finden?

327

328   00:29:15

329   **Lothar Hotz:** Genau, quasi, um da die Datensicherheit zu gewährleisten. Ich meine, das

330   machen sie ja auch schon zum Beispiel in Rechenzentren in Krankenhäusern. Das ist

331   immer komplett getrennt von allen anderen Aktivitäten im Krankenhaus. Also das

332   Rechenzentrum, wo die Patientendaten drin sind. Da gibt es schon

333   Sicherungsmaßnahmen. Letztens wurden ja eben Gesundheitsdaten gestohlen. Das ist das

334   Gebiet der Cybersecurity und nicht direkt der KI sozusagen. Die KI muss das halt erst

335   mal wieder alles entschlüsseln, damit man da etwas mit machen kann.

336

337

338

339   00:30:02

340   **Sina Kiene:** Das heißt, dass wir dann sozusagen drei Schritte benötigen. Man nimmt die
341   Daten auf, sie werden verschlüsselt, dann werden sie entschlüsselt und dann werden sie
342   der KI übergeben.

343

344   00:30:11

345   **Lothar Hotz:** Ja und dann analysiert und wieder verschlüsselt oder so. Es gibt auch
346   Verfahren, die versuchen mit verschlüsselten Daten irgendetwas zu machen. Das heißt,
347   an der Stelle benutzt man Cybersecurity, dann KI-Verfahren oder so. Aber es ist natürlich
348   schon eine Gefahr.

349

350   00:30:44

351   **Sina Kiene:** Vielen Dank, dass Sie sich Zeit für mich genommen habe, um meine Fragen
352   zu KI-Systemen zu beantworten. Einen schönen Abend noch für Sie.

353

YOUR KNOWLEDGE HAS VALUE

- We will publish your bachelor's and master's thesis, essays and papers

- Your own eBook and book - sold worldwide in all relevant shops

- Earn money with each sale

Upload your text at www.GRIN.com and publish for free